THAT'S
BIG

THAT'S BIG

Believing It's God!

ELIZABETH A. WILLIAMS

XULON PRESS

Xulon Press
2301 Lucien Way #415
Maitland, FL 32751
407.339.4217
www.xulonpress.com

That's BIG: *Believing It's God!*
© 2022 by Elizabeth A. Williams

All rights reserved solely by the author. The author guarantees all contents are original and do not infringe upon the legal rights of any other person or work. No part of this book may be reproduced in any form without the permission of the author.

Due to the changing nature of the Internet, if there are any web addresses, links, or URLs included in this manuscript, these may have been altered and may no longer be accessible. The views and opinions shared in this book belong solely to the author and do not necessarily reflect those of the publisher. The publisher therefore disclaims responsibility for the views or opinions expressed within the work.

Cover design: MindingYourLiz

Author photo: Brooke Glassford/Colorbox

Unless otherwise indicated, Scripture quotations taken from the King James Version (KJV) – *public domain.*

Paperback ISBN-13: 978-1-6628-5659-4
Ebook ISBN-13: 978-1-6628-5660-0

This book is dedicated to the willing vessel God used on April 29, 1996 to give me an amazing testimony and another chance at life.

Thank you, my real life hero, John Curry.

ACKNOWLEDGEMENTS

All glory to God for paving every step of the way for this book to be written. I was only a willing vessel. *And at times, I wasn't very willing.* God, I thank you for being the author and for using me as your vessel.

John Curry, thank you for allowing God to use you to help save me. Thank you for showing me miracles happen and that God uses us to make them happen. Thank you for blessing me to have a second chance at life and an opportunity to have a testimony to tell the world.

Thank you, Apostle Je'Don Lowe and Prophetess Valerie Johnson-Lowe for always being there for me, especially through this season of my life. You are my spiritual father and mother *(and my favorites)*. Thank you for your continuous love, prayers and support. Thank you for starting 2Gather Ministry during the pandemic. I needed the bible study and the 5 a.m. prayer calls. *It's early, but it's worth it.* Thank you my 2Gather Family.

Thank you, Robert James, my mentor, my Joseph, for having a dream and sharing it with me to push me to heights that I never thought I was capable of reaching. Thank you for boldly telling me to write this book. Thank you for believing in me when I didn't believe in myself.

Thank you, Jillian, Leslie, Melody, Courtney, Robert, and Xavier, for being true friends and so much more. You were the additional people that knew that I was writing. You continued to ask me about the book, *which was probably your way of making sure I was still on task*. Thank you for being there for me throughout the end of this process. Your support has meant so much to me.

Thank you, Pastors Steven and Yolanda Huntley, my beloved pastors at True Divine Baptist Church, for being amazing spiritual leaders. In the last eight years, you've helped me grow spiritually. You have both seen gifts and talents in me and you wouldn't let me sit on them. Thank you for choosing me as a vessel to help in ministry.

Ma, thank you for every sacrifice you made for me. There are a lot of difficult truths in this book, but when it comes down to it, I know you love me and you did the best you could for me. I will always love you.

Dad, thank you for being true to who you are. At times, we are definitely two peas in the same pod. *Thanks for being okay with me putting your business in the street.* And for the record, I love you more.

The list of friends, family, co-workers who have helped me is so long. *This is why they say don't start naming people.* Thank you to everyone who has had a part in me becoming who God has created me to be. You have all had purpose and I'm grateful. You all know who you are.

Contents

CHAPTER 1
BIG Miracle 1

CHAPTER 2
BIG Timing 15

CHAPTER 3
BIG Battles 27

CHAPTER 4
BIG Wisdom 41

CHAPTER 5
BIG Plans 55

CHAPTER 6
BIG Love 67

CHAPTER 7
BIG Mercy 83

CHAPTER 8
BIG Healing 99

CHAPTER 9
BIG Forgiveness 113

CHAPTER 10
BIG Identity 131

Afterword 143
About the Author/Vessel 147

INTRODUCTION

AS FAR BACK AS I CAN REMEMBER I HAVE numerous memories of growing up in church. I was born and raised in the South, the Bible Belt. *No one really calls it that anymore, but once the Bible Belt, always the Bible Belt or so I hope.* I am very proud of where I was born and raised. *Wait...maybe not "very proud", but I'm fairly proud of my Southern upbringing.* As I travel around the country and beyond, I have learned that I, as a Southerner, tend to get categorized into this box filled with stereotypes. In this box lie the assumptions that I'm a church-going, pew-hopping, Bible-carrying, WWJD bracelet-wearing religious person with a Southern country accent. And just to let you know I have never hopped a pew. *Not that I would ever admit it.*

The stereotype is somewhat true because I was definitely a church-goer. I remember my mom taking me and my brothers to church every Sunday. I was actually in church every Wednesday. I was in church for every revival. Oh and of course, I was at every Vacation Bible School. *You get it. I was in church a lot. In fact, for my family to not have a car, my mom definitely made sure we got to church.* Church was definitely a priority. I was in church learning. I was in Sunday school, the youth choir, youth plays and programs.

When I was saved at fourteen years old, I was so excited. I understood how important God was to me. I did not fully comprehend what it all truly meant, but I could feel God. He was real to me. I couldn't explain everything that I was feeling, but I knew Christ was living inside of me. I was excited about learning more about my Father, His Son, the Holy Spirit and how I could grow more in my spiritual life. *Some may say, I was not the typical teenager and they would be right.* I was ready to walk out my new Christian life.

And walk out my new Christian life is what I did. Reading about God's promises and provision was exciting. I saw the many benefits of being a Christian and living a Christ-centered life. God was my heavenly Father. My biological father died of cancer when I was too young to remember and besides my mom's boyfriend's I didn't have a real father figure in my house. Once I was saved, God was my Father. I talked to him as if He was right there with me. I was probably a little unrealistic with what all I imagined my life would be after giving it to Christ. Maybe I was the only person who thought that once I gave my life to Christ that I could sing "the storm is over now" and the storm would really be over. Let's remember I was a teenager and a new believer so I had no idea what this new life in Christ was going to be about. *It's called unrealistic expectations.*

Well, let's just say I realized quickly it didn't mean the storms were over or would never come. For me, it sort of meant they were coming and sometimes in full force. Thunderstorms, tornadoes, hurricanes and tsunamis were all right there waiting on me before I could even dry off from being baptized. Things started happening way beyond my understanding and I felt attacked from every direction. *If you're thinking how much attacking can happen to a fourteen year old, just keep reading and you'll see how life drastically changed for me only months after being raised out of the baptismal pool.*

At an early age, I learned that storms came and it didn't always look good or feel good, but it will work out for my good. All the storms would work together for my good. I had to make a choice early in my life to decide whether to believe God or the enemy. I

INTRODUCTION

believed God was with me through everything. *And I mean through everything. And I've been through a lot!* I held on to Him, knowing that He would never leave me or forsake me. When it didn't look good and the enemy was coming from every side, I had to choose to stand on the word of God and know it was going to work out for my good. When I believed and held on to that promise from God, I was able to view life through a different lens, a more optimistic lens. I saw God having an active role in things that happened to me and through me. The way I viewed my life, my experiences, my circumstances made the difference in how I wrote my story and how I lived my life.

The reality is that we all have a story. The way we choose to draw from our story is up to us. I decided everything I had been through in my life was meant to give God glory. He will never get the glory He deserves if I don't tell the story. My story is filled with the enemy wreaking havoc and trying to take me out of the game starting as a teenager. *Now that I'm thinking about it, I wouldn't be surprised if there was some story about my umbilical cord being wrapped around my neck. The enemy might have tried to take me out in the womb. Who knows!*

I know the enemy has been continuously attacking my mind and body while aiming for my soul all my life. The enemy would want nothing better than for me to be defeated. The thing about it is that with every attack, I began to see how God had an intricate part in using the attacks to mold me, to strengthen me, to teach me. I believed that God was using everything in my life for His purpose. I began to ask myself some questions. What do I do with my story of God's grace, mercy and unconditional love? What do I do when God is telling me to be transparent and tell the story?

A couple of years ago, I was listening to a worship song on YouTube that led me to listening to a sermon from a pastor at a church in North Carolina which led me to listening to a message from a pastor at a church in Oklahoma. In that message, the pastor used an acronym that changed my life. He said HOT (Honest, Open, and Transparent). I began to embrace it. I realized I was going to live by this acronym. I had to be HOT! God was calling me to be honest, open and transparent. *I'll take that call over some of the other ones. Definitely glad I wasn't called to be a pastor.*

That sermon led me to a church in Denver where a young woman began to speak into my life. The trials she had faced at such an early age made me look at my own life and see what God's purpose was for me. I found myself listening to her messages daily. She pulled me in when we had the same attitude towards Eve. She kept saying write the book. The messages would be different but she kept saying write the book. I felt like she was speaking to me. I felt like God was speaking to me through this woman of God. How had one worship song on YouTube led me all the way to this place that I honestly didn't want to be at? *Thanks a lot, YouTube Autoplay.*

I knew it was God speaking. I had attempted to write a book about a decade ago and it did not go well. *Horrible attempt!* I didn't make it past a couple of paragraphs on a sheet of paper. *There's absolutely no telling where that paper is.* Honestly, I didn't really want to write, but I needed to be obedient. I couldn't avoid it this time. I had grown in my relationship with God. I had matured spiritually thanks to great spiritual leaders. Different pastors, different sermons and messages, but I received the same word from God. My message kept being the same. There was no doubt there were two things I was meant to do: be HOT and write a book.

Well, almost two years later, I finally became obedient. It took one of my mentors telling me he had a dream about me. *You already know what happened in the dream.* I was writing a book! *He just couldn't keep that dream to himself.* I could not keep running from

INTRODUCTION

what God told me to do. I wasn't telling God no this time. I was just prolonging the process. *Don't act like you never took your sweet little time when God told you to do something. Well, maybe you haven't, but I'm definitely guilty.* For me, I needed several confirmations before I walked into what God placed in my heart. This book was definitely in my heart. It is an untold story that had to be told. Maya Angelou said, "There is no agony like bearing an untold story inside of you." I have chosen to have freedom from this agony. I'm telling my story.

I am a believer who strives to be obedient. *I did say strive so I'm not always successful, as you will read.* But I am giving you what God has shown me in my life. There are particular events and experiences in my life that are quite unique and divine. There are things that took place in my life that I did not think would ever happen to me. I could not have ever dreamed or imagined. Some of those things were by my own doing and some were at the hands of others. Whether by my hand or others, God has used every event as testimonies throughout my life. Through every situation in my life, good or bad, God has used it to bless me and even others. I'm a work in progress, but I'm a willing vessel ready to tell the world that I believe it is God who has worked and is working in my life.

As I confess that I am a work in progress, I also want it to be known that I consider myself witty. While others have called me sarcastic or even a tad bit petty – I know they mean it in the nicest way possible. *So call me Petty LaBelle, Petty White, Petty Wop or whatever petty name you can find.* I'd like to believe the life I've lived so far gives me a pass for finding humor in almost everything. *I'm totally stretching with that. Or am I?* I do feel like God has a sense of humor though and that helps me own every bit of who I am.

My name is Elizabeth Williams, I love God, I love Jesus and I can be a little sarcastic and petty at times. The personal accounts in this book are definitely not about a perfect person, but about someone who definitely changed through the perfect sacrifice, Jesus Christ. These events in my life all point to how I decided to see God in every situation no matter if it was good or bad, happy or sad, joyful or painful. This story is about someone who chooses to believe that God is always present, always working in each of our lives. This book is about how my faith in God changed my whole perspective, my whole outlook on life, just by choosing to believe it's God.

Now, let's get to the BIG story.

Chapter 1

BIG MIRACLE

"Officer, unknown man pluck teen from sunken car" was the headline of the local newspaper when I made the front page. Really? Pluck? *Believe it.* That was the title an editor decided to splash on the front page. *Just a shame!* It's not the title I would have picked and it is grammatically incorrect, but at least I made the newspaper. *It's not exactly the way I wanted to end up in the headlines, but beggars can't be choosy.* I guess two local writers heard about my traumatic car accident that happened two days earlier and decided that I was newsworthy. It was too bad that I was unconscious when I became locally famous. *Who am I kidding? We all know that if the off-duty officer had not been involved, my story, well my name would have never made it to that paper.* I wasn't exactly famous, but to my friends, family, classmates and church members I was the center of attention at least for a little while. It had been two days of battling for my life and I was finally in stable condition. I was unconscious, but stable. *I took what I could get at the time.*

I know it must have been hard for my loved ones to come to the intensive care unit and sit around my bed waiting for me to wake up day after day. The good news is that the day came. I mean the day came seven days later, but the day came that I regained consciousness. The car accident I was involved in happened on a Monday and I woke up the following Monday. I ended up being unconscious for seven days. Yes, seven days! *I tell people I talk a lot because I'm making up for the whole seven days I lost. You can laugh. God will have to tell me Himself that He doesn't have a sense of humor. I believe He is a comical genius to allow me to be unconscious, unable to speak for seven days. Come on!*

Now waking up in a hospital in the intensive care unit was a little much for me. I didn't know what day it was. I had no idea what happened. I had no idea why I was there. I just woke up and I couldn't remember anything. I didn't feel any pain. To be honest, I couldn't feel anything. I couldn't do much. I just laid there helpless and disoriented. The small thing I could do though is reach my right hand to my head and feel a little bit of hair. What did I do that for? It completely went wrong from there as I freaked out about my hair being shaved off. My hair was gone. They basically shaved my head. It wasn't even cut in a hairstyle. It was just patchy and bald. *I had a meltdown. It is amazing the things that make people anxious and worried.* I didn't remember any pain at that moment or anything other than my crown and glory was gone. I was sitting in the intensive care unit upset about my hair, not knowing a week earlier I basically died and came back. I had no comprehension of what happened to me. I did not understand what happened to my hair.

My oldest brother who didn't even live in the state anymore was at my bedside. *He was so over the dirty South. He never came home. Was it that serious that my brother came to town to see me?* My brother began to tell me about what happened. As he talked, I began to cry. As he explained I had been in a car accident where the car went off the road into a creek, I could not stop crying. Every detail was unbelievable. It was an unexplainable "thank you God" cry. My attention turned from my hair to asking myself, how was I even alive. In true big brother style, he decided to lighten the mood by telling me all the times he beat me up when we were little kids made me tough enough to survive the accident. It took my mind off of things for just a moment. The next moment though, I thought, "Wait, why can't I move the left side of my body?"

It turned out that I was involved in a really bad car accident and my neck was broken in the process of the car flipping off the road and landing into a creek. My broken neck caused me to suffer nerve damage to my left side. *If you think I freaked out about my hair, you should have been there when I couldn't move my left side.* I had semi-paralysis on my left side and no one could determine when or if I would regain the use of that side of my body. My arm and leg just laid there motionless. After hearing each devastating detail of this traumatic accident that I had survived, I was in total disbelief. I knew I served a God that could do anything but this was really unbelievable. What my brother was explaining to me made no sense. I couldn't remember anything though. Why couldn't I remember anything?

I went to school the day of the accident. It took a moment, but I did remember it rained all day. It was a rainy Monday. It was the type of day I disliked with a passion. I disliked rainy days for a very good and valid reason, my hair. *Well, at that moment I didn't have the hair problem anymore.* The little I remembered happened the week before. Remember, I lost seven days of my life. *Hence the reason why I talk so much! Just remember making up for lost time.* Don't get me wrong I was grateful to be alive, but I literally lost seven days of my life I could never get back. *Do you know how long seven days is to a freshman in high school? Really long!*

I was puzzled over the events of the accident. I was at a loss for words. I was even more at a loss for words when my neurologist explained my injuries to me in full detail. *So many details and long* words! *As if I understood medical terminology at the time. It took me getting my medical records later in life to somewhat understand that entire lingo.* He explained to me that I had head and spinal injuries. I had suffered a broken neck and it was severe. It turned out that two vertebrae in my neck, C4 and C5, were damaged, which turned out to mean crushed. They had to be replaced. The neurosurgeon had no choice but to do a fusion to fix the broken bones. If you're like me, I didn't know what a fusion was. *Well not until after I had to have one.* For those who don't know, a fusion is when they join two vertebrae with a bone graft held together with hardware. The bone graft joins the vertebrae above and below to form one solid piece of bone. *Yes, I have a neck of steel. Superhuman, some would say! Just kidding.*

    I had to wear a heavy, painful halo that was screwed into my head to keep my neck aligned. *Don't imagine the angelic halo. And, I don't know why I'm saying wear it like it was a tiara or something.* Let's also remember that besides the broken neck, adding to the severity of my injuries was the amount of time that I was submerged underwater. When I arrived at the hospital, my mom was told that there was a chance that I may not make it and if I did, I may have brain damage. I know they have to prepare you for the worst case scenario but what a pill to swallow. I was told that my mom, church members, family and friends surrounded my hospital bed and prayed for me. Pray without ceasing is what they did for me. When I couldn't pray for myself, they did. I believe this made all the difference when I was unconscious and fighting to survive.

    I needed to know more about the day of the accident. I needed to know more. Where were we coming from? Why were we on that road? It turned out that after school, I was babysitting my godsister who was eleven years old at the time. I often watched her for my godmother. *Now that I think about it, was it technically babysitting if I didn't get paid? It was more like I was "voluntold" to do something. I didn't volunteer and I didn't receive compensation for keeping her so let's stick with "voluntold".* My seventeen year old brother usually helped me out at times especially if my godmother was out of town. *He definitely wasn't compensated.*

My brother's friend would pick us up and take us where we needed to go. Man, when we saw that Nissan Maxima drive up, we acted as if he was our personal chauffeur. That evening we were going to my mom's apartment to get some clothes for my brother who decided to stay with us since my godmother wasn't getting in until the following day. We made it safely to my mom's apartment which was about four miles away from my godmother's house. When we headed back things took a drastic turn for the worse.

We rode down a familiar road that we always took. It was a road that we had just taken earlier that evening. The road had an overpass over a small shallow creek and was exactly 0.9 miles away from my godmother's house. *Yes, I know it down to a tee because I've calculated it, dreamed of it and driven it multiple times over the past years.* Driving down that dark, wet road, my brother's friend lost control of the car while going around the curve. Before we made it to the overpass, he ran off the road and into the creek. The car flipped a couple of times and landed upside down into the water. Now on an average day, this shallow creek barely had water in it. *I don't know which one would have been better, water or no water.* The creek was the complete opposite of shallow that night because it had been raining all day long.

On that non-stop rainy Monday, the creek was filled. I'm only 5'3.7 (*every bit counts*), so it was well above my head if I was standing in the creek. Standing is something that I wished I could have been doing at that time as I remained in the passenger seat. I have often heard that the passenger seat is the worst seat to be in during an accident. *I've personally always thought that any seat is the worst seat in an accident.* As I hung upside down in the car, I became a believer about the front passenger seat that night.

I always hopped in the front seat of a car. I guess I was just happy to be riding instead of walking since we didn't have a car. My brother and godsister were in the back seat of the car. Everyone got out of the car, except for me. My godsister ended up getting out the trunk. *Don't ask me how.* My brother and his friend got out but I was trapped. *Nobody was hurt but me. Lucky me!* Not only was I trapped but to make matters worse, I was underwater. Time was of the essence as I remained in the seat of the car, submerged underwater with a broken neck.

There were townhouses located directly across from the street where the accident took place. People literally heard the accident and by this time they came out of their houses to see what was going on. Even though I don't know the exact number of people who were standing around asking what was going on, I know one thing for sure. As I was trapped in the car underwater and unconscious, none of them came into the water to help me. The onlookers were just standing around asking questions and *obviously* just looking. I learned that night that it only takes one onlooker to make all the difference. God! He sits high and looks down low. I believe God intervened and everything changed for my good. He began to set things into motion that saved my life that night.

A twenty-four year old off-duty officer took that road and went that way that specific night. He didn't usually go that way to get home. *When God is involved though! Don't make me shout!* He picked up his four year old son and was headed home. When he was driving by on that dark, rainy night, he saw several people along the road by the overpass and the creek. He stopped on the right side of the road and told his young son to stay in the truck. The off-duty officer left his crying son in the car and came across the street to the accident scene. He started asking the people standing along the bank what happened and what was going on. *Might I add these were the same people that weren't helping and just looking, as I was drowning in a car!* People were yelling "help, she's trapped in the car" and he immediately reacted. The officer got into the water. He saw my foot hanging out of the window. He began trying to pull me out of the window of the car. I wouldn't budge. I was stuck on something. He continued to pull me and I wouldn't budge.

Some other man that came to help asked the officer what he could do. The off-duty officer told him to try to push while he would pull me. With one push from this stranger, my body loosened and I was free to be pulled out. *Majority of the people that I share my testimony with tell me that the stranger that we haven't been able to find was my guardian angel. I say, you better believe he was.* Psalm 91:11 says, "For he shall give his angels charge over thee, to keep thee in all thy ways." I was guarded that night. Do I believe in angels? Yes, I do. Do I believe that there are heavenly beings that God places in the earth realm to do his work and be his vessels? Yes, I do. *Everyone has a right to their opinion but as for me, I was definitely made a believer.*

The off-duty officer carried me out of the water and laid me on the ground onto the bank of the creek. He was about to do CPR when I coughed up some water and began breathing. After that moment I lost consciousness. *What the what! After basically drowning, the police officer never even did CPR on me. After being underwater for all that time, he never performed CPR. No chest compressions. No rescue breaths. What in the world!* I have never been able to explain that. I have just added it to the list of absolutely unexplainable, divine moments where God intervened. I learned a lot about His sovereignty in that one night. He was absolutely totally, completely in control that night.

At this point, some of you may be thinking this is a fiction book. *It's okay. I'm used to it.* Let me assure you that as unrealistic as this accident sounds, it is quite true. I do not remember the accident. I do not even remember the entire day, which my neurologist said was a good thing because it was extremely traumatic. I do know that everything that was told to me is true. It's just flat out unexplainable to me but it definitely happened. I have questioned the accident and the entire day more times than I can count. I could question it all I wanted to, but the reality is that I have a huge scar on my neck along with numerous scars on my body, newspaper articles, local news stories, medical records and not to mention several witnesses as proof that it definitely happened. *Yes, I felt like I needed to explain that at that moment. I mean, no CPR after being underwater that long...absolutely unbelievable, miraculous.*

An ambulance arrived and took me to the hospital where I had to fight to survive. Even in being transported to the hospital, God was not done intervening. *Let me explain.* You see, the accident took place less than half a mile from a hospital. Instead of taking me to the hospital that was practically right there, I was taken to the hospital across town. When I was told this, you know that it made absolutely no sense to me. *If I was conscious, I could've ran from the accident scene to the hospital. That's exactly how close it was.* With a hospital being that close, why would I be taken across town? *It's not like the ambulance gets paid by the miles traveled.* Why would they take me to a hospital that was 9.9 miles away? Why? *I'm glad you asked.* Well, the hospital across town was where one of the best neurosurgeons was working that night. *I don't know who made that decision in the natural, but I believe God supernaturally sent me to that hospital.* That neurosurgeon worked with numerous trauma patients. God used that neurosurgeon to help save my life. The details of my accident that made absolutely no sense to me began to make sense as I began to see God working things out for my good. As I began to believe that it was God helping me, I could see that it was God working a miracle.

I was discharged from the hospital after two weeks. Yes, only two weeks in the hospital. I was unconscious for half of the time so it went by quickly even though it seemed like forever. Believe it or not, I walked out. *Well, you know they have to push you out in the wheelchair...but then I walked. It's all in the details, people!* I got out of the wheelchair with no assistance. I guess I should rewind to let you know that I started walking in the hospital. The good news was that the nerve damage affected my left arm more than my left leg. *Don't ask. You know I cannot explain it. And to say "good news" is kinda stretching it. My left arm was still just there, motionless.* I do know one thing for sure. I had days of excruciating walks in the hospital that more than likely assisted with me being able to walk. All of those walks were assisted by wonderful nurses and therapists that I'm forever indebted to. There is something about God touching you through the hands of healthcare workers. I know that He was ever so present in every heartfelt smile, encouraging word and loving touch.

The locally famous miracle teenager was headed home. My mom's apartment was right around the corner from my high school. People were constantly coming by to check on me. I was so self-conscious about how I looked. My hair was bald and patchy. My left arm would just lay motionless. I had visible scars on my face, my hands and my left shoulder. The worst part was my eyes were red. The sclera, *you know the white part of an eye,* was red. Every time I looked in the mirror, I wanted to cry. And more times than I would like to admit to it, I did cry. *I looked like a red eyed dragon or something.* There were times when I was feeling really bad about myself. After all God had spared me from, I would still have bad days. Days of pain, days of frustration, days of doubt, but God was so faithful. He always placed someone there to give me an encouraging word. He even helped me encourage myself.

Remember that newspaper article; well it became a physical reminder of my accident. I would read it often. Going home and reading that article made things even more real. Written in that newspaper was a quote that I couldn't get out of my head. It said "Elizabeth's head was underwater for perhaps five to ten minutes". I still couldn't believe it. It completely explained my hideous red eyes though. Each time I was told details about my accident felt like the first time I was hearing them.

Several years later, I talked to the officer who helped save me, my real life hero, and he told me that I had to have been underwater for longer than ten minutes. He told me that calculating the time he got there, him talking to his son to calm him down, coming across to the scene and then trying to get me out would equate to longer than ten minutes. *I completely take his word for it.* He remembered my accident like it was yesterday. How did I find the police officer to talk to him? *I'm glad you asked.*

Ten years after my accident, I was getting married. *That's a chapter all by itself. You'll get there.* The local news station that covered my accident in 1996 decided to do a story on my search to find the police officer and the unknown man who helped save me. My mom never searched for either of them to even say thank you. I wanted to thank them personally and invite them to my wedding. The news station interviewed me at my office. About a week later, I found out that they found the police officer. I went to the news station and had my first conversation with my hero. His ex-wife saw the news story and contacted the station. He was being deployed so we could only talk on the phone. It was one of the best conversations of my life as I cried on television talking to a man that God used to save me. To this day, we still haven't been able to find the unknown man. *But you know how I feel about that. Definitely my guardian angel!*

It is still unbelievable to me that I was underwater for such a long amount of time. Have you ever held your breath to see how long you can hold your breath? *I don't really think that people sit around doing that but who knows.* Well, I have done it and to this day, my record is forty-four seconds. *I guess when it counted the most; I came through like a champ.* Seriously though, I knew that God intervened. He showed up in multiple ways during and after my accident.

I survived being underwater for about ten minutes, with a broken neck and pneumonia. How do you even comprehend that? It was completely beyond my understanding. Not only had I survived but I was thriving. There was no doubt that I was extremely blessed. My life had definitely been spared. A few years after my accident, a close friend of mine was killed in a car accident. His car ran off the road and hit a tree. He was killed instantly. I questioned how I was still alive and he wasn't. My accident seemed so much worse than his. His life was taken and mine was spared. Why? I don't know. Some things are beyond my comprehension. *A lot of things are beyond my comprehension and understanding.*

I knew I was alive for everyone to see God's power. I was alive for people to see that God is the same God, yesterday, today and forevermore. When people found out about my accident, they wanted to know more about it. Bold strangers would see the scar on my neck and ask me what happened. *I don't care if you ask, but just don't touch my neck. That's creepy.* Yes, people have done it on more than one occasion. I loved sharing the details of my accident with others. I could only tell them what I knew. I knew that God worked a miracle that rainy Monday night. I was literally known as the miracle child in the intensive care unit.

My accident was a topic that I couldn't get away from and neither did I want to. I was alive to tell the story. God knew that I would tell everybody about what happened to me. If you look at me now, you cannot tell what I've been through. *I'm sure a lot of us can say that.* There are still so many questions that I don't have answers to, even after all these years. Questions like: What happened to that stranger that helped the officer? Why couldn't we ever find him? How was I underwater for so long and I didn't drown? Why didn't I suffer brain damage from being submerged underwater for the amount of time that the newspaper, police officer and witnesses said? Why wasn't I paralyzed from my neck down? How in the world did I survive? My answer to all the questions is the same.

I decided to go with one thing and I stand firmly on it. I believe it's God. There are still so many unknowns but I know that I serve an all-knowing Father who sits high and looks low. I believe that His intervention made the difference in me surviving that car accident. If you ask me, is there anything too hard for God, my answer will always and forever be a resounding "NO". I wholeheartedly believe that nothing is impossible with God. That's what He does...He creates possibilities. He does the unexplainable, the BIG miracles.

> And Jesus looking upon them saith, With men it is impossible, but not with God: for with God all things are possible. ~Mark 10:27 KJV

> Then said Jesus unto him, Except ye see signs and wonders, ye will not believe. ~John 4:48

DO ME A FAVOR

Look back over your life and think about something that happened to you that's just unexplainable. You can't explain how. You can't quite put it into words or maybe you can. Maybe your bill was due and the money showed up. *I've been there a time or two or three or four.* Maybe you were told you couldn't have a baby and you finally saw a positive sign on your pregnancy test. Maybe you survived an accident, illness or disease that some people didn't survive. That's BIG. Believe it's God that worked on your behalf in the situation. Learn to identify and celebrate your BIG miracles. Give God praise for working on your behalf. Take a moment right now and thank God for blessing you.

Now go one more step, think of someone that you can be a blessing to and go be their miracle. God uses us to bless others. He uses us to make miracles happen for other people. My story would be so different if the off-duty police officer and random stranger had not been willing vessels. They are my heroes that God used. A hero doesn't have to literally physically save someone's life. You can make an impact in numerous ways in someone's life and that can make you their hero. Go be a hero. Go be a blessing. Go be a miracle. Remember nothing is impossible when God is involved.

PRAY WITH ME

Father God, you are the King of Kings, the Lord of Lords, Jehovah Jireh, our provider, Jehovah Rapha, our healer. You are the great I Am. We thank you God for showing us your power. When things seem impossible, we can lean and depend on you knowing that you can and will make a way. Thank you for building our faith. You said in your word that we only need faith the size of a mustard seed and we're thankful that our faith is growing more and more each day. You specialize in making a way out of no way and we thank you.

When people say "no way", circumstances say "no, that's impossible", God you say "yes, I am that I am". Teach us to see all the miracles that you are continuously doing in our lives. Thank you Father for showing us that miracles come in all different ways and that there is nothing that you cannot do when we, your children, believe. When challenges arise, help us to think back on the times that you, our heavenly Father, have made a way out of no way. Help us to recall your goodness. Help us to know that you will never leave us or forsake us. You are an ever present help in the time of need. Thank you, Father, for being a miracle-working, good, good Father. In the name of Jesus, we pray. Amen.

Chapter 2

BIG TIMING

THERE'S SOMETHING THAT I NEVER SAID OUT loud that I am about to tell you and I'm prepared for any judging that comes along with it. Here we go! After surviving a very traumatic car accident, I felt like God would answer any prayer that I lifted up to Him. I felt like He was attentive to me. Not like God was my personal genie and would make my wishes come true. *Oh, that sounds so bad when I say it out loud.* I meant more like He heard my prayers and would definitely answer them. I thought based upon God sparing my life in a miraculous way that it meant He was on my side and literally I could ask and it would be done. Matthew 7:7 says "Ask and it will be given to you; seek and you will find; knock and the door will be opened to you." *I was taking that scripture to a whole new level. I was still new in my walk with Christ.* I was still on spiritual milk and would run with a scripture and shape it to mean what I needed it to be. Who wouldn't in my situation, though? I had defied the odds. In fact, I had defied every single, last odd.

God worked a miracle in my life and I was enjoying every moment of being the miracle teenager. I had a second chance at life. At a young age I had been so blessed to see the hand of God in my own life. There is a complete difference between my mom talking about how good God was, my pastor preaching about miracles, a friend telling me about how God made a way in their life and actually experiencing it all for myself. I was living proof that miracles happen. *Oh, you couldn't tell me anything.* Being humble was one of the many things that I had to learn after my accident. I thought very highly of myself because I was a survivor. *That was a good enough reason for me.* I was a bald head, neck brace wearing, ambitious Christian young lady who was ready for whatever was next. I honestly thought I was ready. Ready or not, the next step came. It was time to get back to my normal teenage life. It was time to conquer therapy.

Due to my injuries, I had to go through speech therapy, occupational therapy and physical therapy. The first day I went to therapy, they realized that the speech therapy was not needed. I was in there talking the speech therapist's head off. She knew all about my accident by the time I left that session. She probably felt like she heard a sermon because I talked extensively about God. *Come on now, less than a month ago, my neck had been broken, I had pneumonia, I was unconscious for seven days. Oh and let's not forget that I was trapped in a car and was underwater for about ten minutes.* I couldn't explain how I survived that accident without talking extensively about God. Let's just say she received a whole earful. The speech therapist politely told me that I was not required to come back for speech therapy. *Now that I think about it, was it because I didn't need it or she just didn't want me to talk her ear off again. Who knows!*

Occupational therapy was a little more difficult though. I still suffered semi-paralysis to my left side. It only affected my arm at that point but a nerve-damaged left arm made life a little difficult. I could brush my teeth but not tie my shoe. I could brush my short hair but if it had been longer, I couldn't have put it in a ponytail. *Yes, I'm being a little petty. I missed my hair.* My arm just laid there motionless which was so frustrating. My neurologist explained how the nerves could repair themselves in time. There were no signs of anything happening with that arm.

I was definitely blessed though because I was able to do daily functions. I knew exactly what it meant when people said you don't miss something until it's gone. For a sixteen year old who wanted to go back to school with as much normalcy as possible, it was nerve wracking. *No pun intended.* As much as I was thinking negative thoughts, I still saw God in this bad situation. I realized that even in this situation I chose to believe it was God that allowed it to be my left arm instead of my right arm, which was my dominant arm. *You gotta love that positive thinking.* The truth was that it could have been so much worse than what I was dealing with. I could brush my teeth. I could write. I could feed myself. I couldn't lose hope. I had to believe that God was going to restore the nerves and motion in my arm. I had to make the most out of the situation I was in.

I was alive. I was grateful. I was making the most out of the situation but for the record, physical therapy was the worst. I was alive and well, but I was miserable. I shouldn't have had the audacity to complain, but I did. I was nowhere and no how prepared for physical therapy. I had to do these exercises that would hurt so badly. *If you have ever had to go to physical therapy, you feel my pain. If you're going through physical therapy right now, just hang in there. I wish someone had told me that.*

I remember this one exercise where the therapist would lay my arm on the wall and he or she would keep moving it up as high as they could. They were stretching it. It was the most excruciating pain. *I'm having flashbacks right now.* I would often think that if I can't move my arm, why could I feel this pain in my shoulder? My left shoulder had this huge scar on it. I call it one of my many war wounds from glass slicing and dicing me as the car flipped a couple of times before landing in that creek. This scar made matters worse for my left arm. Let me just tell you I had to push through every day. There is a song I used to sing that talks about encouraging yourself in the Lord. Let me just tell you I needed more than myself. The encouragement was done. I wanted to keep singing that song but it was a wrap.

What does a sixteen year old who didn't know how important physical therapy was to repairing nerve damage and successfully recovering do? What happens when a sixteen year old does not know any better and does not feel like going to physical therapy sessions that make her hurt even worse? Well, I quit physical therapy. No one told me "quitters never win", "don't give up", "you'll regret it". Nope, not one person forced me to continue physical therapy. *Special thanks to my family and friends that let me quit. Good looking out for a sista! I love you, but you should've pushed me.*

I think that it was so easy for me to quit for two reasons though. One reason was that everyone worshiped the ground I walked on. *I wish there was another way to say that but at this moment there is not*. Everyone was so happy that I survived an extremely traumatic, life threatening accident. My mom was not going to make me do anything I did not want to do. The baby of the family and her only daughter could get away with anything at that point. *I really hope she doesn't read this part. She may not want to read this at all. Sorry, Ma!* I tried to not test her to see if I could really get away with anything.

Speaking of my mom, she's the other reason why I could quit with ease. Like I said before, my mom didn't own a car. She didn't own a car because she never, *I mean never* learned how to drive. I guess she never had a desire to. I was told that one time she attempted to drive my grandfather's car and never made it out the driveway. Why would my grown mother be convinced to drive when she knew she didn't know how to? Even worse, she was convinced by my older brother who was maybe nine years old at the time. He so-call coached her. *Yes, this already sounds bad.* The end result was what we all could have guessed. She actually ran into her parent's brick house. I have never talked to my mom about that but my brother and cousin have told the story numerous times. *If it's not true, when she reads this she'll set me straight and probably hit me for putting her business in the street.*

My mom would have to get someone to pick us up for me to even go to my physical therapy sessions. When I decided I had endured enough pain from my accident and refused to continue this trauma through therapy, my mom didn't care. The rehabilitation center was one less destination to hitch a ride to. *Why didn't I come up with Uber? Most of my childhood was spent walking. We walked to church, walked to school, walked to the store. To this day, I'm surprised that I voluntarily started running and walking recreationally. I guess all those childhood years were training me to run 5Ks and marathons. Maybe I did suffer some brain damage from being underwater.*

So now I was a quitter who still had to do the physical therapy exercises at home. The exercises still hurt at home. It did not matter where I did them. I still hated them. Hate is such a strong word and I do not use it often but it is warranted when discussing my physical therapy. So what did I do? I quit again. At this point, there was no progress. There was still no sign of my arm improving. My arm just hung there motionless. In my mind, I was thinking this arm may never work again but in my spirit, I believed God for yet another miracle. Remember that I was still thinking that whatever I asked God for in the name of Jesus, he would hear my prayer and answer.

Answering was not what he was doing at all. In fact, I'm pretty sure that God went completely silent on me. The waiting was absolutely no joke. I know that I talked to God about my arm. I know that He heard my prayers. I believed that He heard my prayers. Why wasn't he answering? The waiting, the waiting and waiting was excruciating. I was trying to keep my faith that God would do just as He said He would do but it was hard. He was my healer. He was Jehovah Rapha. I felt like I knew this better than anyone. I had this wonderful testimony to look back on and be reminded of His great miraculous power but at times that didn't matter. At times, some negative thoughts arose.

It seemed like God was not going to answer my prayer. I wanted to keep believing. I wanted to believe that I would use my left arm again. What do you do when you don't see any sign of God doing what He said He would do? My answer was to keep praying, keep waiting, keep believing, and keep trusting. The race is not given to the swift or to the strong but to the one who endures to the end. The truth was that it was a blessing just for me to be in the race. I definitely had to put things in perspective.

Growing up, I would not say I was a very patient person. I do not remember a lot about myself prior to my car accident. *I was more than likely impatient before, after and during that time.* I missed out on being anxious for nothing. I was anxious over almost everything for several years of my life. When I say several, I mean until a couple of years ago. *Let's remember that this is a judgment free zone.* I was often worrying and that led me to being impatient about the outcome. I am a planner by nature. *Also known as a control freak but tomato, to-mah-to. I own it all.* I like having things done and I am constantly checking things off my list. I was anxiously waiting for my arm to regain its use. I was ready to check this off my list so that I could say that I was fully healed from my accident. School was starting back in a few weeks and I needed this situation, this left arm to be properly functioning.

God my healer and provider did what he does best. He did what no one else could do. He worked yet another miracle on my behalf. The miracle actually happened a little over three months after my accident and a couple of weeks before school started. *As a teenager, those months seemed like forever but let me just tell you that as an adult I can only hope that God would do some things so quickly.* I woke up one morning about the second week of August and I raised my left arm. *Sorry, but that's what I got for you.* The truth is I do not know why but I woke up that morning and I attempted to raise my arm.

There is no fancy, dramatic way to describe what happened. *You know if there was a way, I would definitely use it. I never miss an opportunity to be dramatic.* I was lying down and I just lifted up my left arm. I tried lifting this arm morning after morning with no positive result, but I guess the nerves finally got their act together. The nerves repaired themselves with obviously little to no help from me. To this day, I really can't explain it. My arm showed no signs of being repaired. I went to bed the night before with no motion in my arm. I know it was not working. There was no gradual improvement where I could move it even a little. There was no movement at all when I went to sleep the night before. I honestly think that it was truly God's timing.

I had to learn that it was not that God did not hear my prayers but that he would answer in His timing. It's not easy for me to always accept that. To be completely honest, during the waiting period, I'm battling with all types of negative thoughts. I am literally trying to hold on to my faith and hope. I am trying to believe that God will do what He said He would do. In those times, I have to remember John 11 where Lazarus was sick. *Lazarus was sick, sick.* They sent for Jesus and it seemed like Jesus just took His time getting there.

Martha and Mary were waiting on Jesus to come heal their brother. And where was Jesus? He was healing all these other people on the journey to Lazarus. Lazarus ended up dying four days before Jesus got there. *I won't even speak for them, but I would've been giving Jesus the side eye. I would have been real petty. Like Jesus, why did it take you so long? Jesus, you couldn't get here any sooner? Jesus, you can turn back around because He's dead now. Jesus, what held you up this time? Oh okay, so you decided to keep healing people on your way!* Something miraculous happens though. While people are crying and probably upset, Jesus raises Lazarus from the dead. It doesn't matter how it looks. When Jesus arrives and steps on the scene, nothing is impossible. It was His timing. God's perfect timing.

When I think about God's timing, I can't help but think about how my mom, family and friends stood around my bed as I laid there unconscious in that intensive care unit. I can imagine them all waiting for me to wake up, waiting on me to gain consciousness not knowing if I would. Not knowing if I did wake up if I would have brain damage or paralysis. And just like that God touched my body and I woke up with the activity of my limbs *(on one side)* and in my right mind *(at least I claim it to be so)*. I'm sure that they stood around praying, not seeing any change day after day until God's timing happened. He worked a miracle in His timing.

When it looked like all hope was gone and there was no improvement, God decided to step in once again and do yet another miracle in my life. I went to sleep that August night and my arm was dead. I woke up and it was alive. While I was sleeping, God was working. He worked on my behalf. I believe that it was God's timing and not my timing. When it's God's timing, He's never wrong. When He does that thing that we've prayed for, He answers in a way that you cannot deny that it was God and God all alone. It is in His divine timing that things fall into place. Situations are changed.

Dead things and situations rise again. He does it in His perfect, BIG timing.

> For the vision is yet for an appointed time, but at the end it shall speak, and not lie: though it tarry, wait for it; because it will surely come, it will not tarry. ~Habakkuk 2:3 KJV

> Be careful for nothing; but in everything by prayer and supplication with thanksgiving let your requests be made known unto God. ⁷And the peace of God, which passeth all understanding, shall keep your hearts and minds through Christ Jesus. ~Philippians 4:6-7 KJV

DO ME A FAVOR

Think about a time that your timing didn't quite line up with God's timing. How did you feel? Did you get discouraged? Did you doubt that God was going to do what He said He would do? Did you think that maybe you didn't even hear what you thought God was telling you that He would do? And you just waited, you waited, you waited. If you're currently in a season of waiting for God to do something in your life, pray for patience and keep believing. Recall a time in your life when you prayed and God answered you. Remember the times that He did just what He said He would do even when it was not on your timetable. Remember that though it lingers, it will surely come to pass. One of the things that I love about my heavenly Father is that he is not a man, that He will lie. If He said it, He will do it. The process, the delay, the waiting does not mean that the door is closed or that the prayer won't be answered. In those times we should keep our eyes fixed and focused on God. Do not be distracted by how long it's taking for God to do something. Do not allow doubt to surface. If He did it before, He will do it again because God does not change. He's the same today, tomorrow and forever more. It will be His timing and His alone. I can hear and see my mom dressed in her cream and green choir robe standing in the choir stand singing an old gospel song that says, "He may not come when you want Him but He'll be there exactly on time! I tell you He's an on-time God. Yes, He is." If you're asking this popular question: Lord when? Just know that His timing is PERFECT! When you're getting weary from waiting, keep your faith in God. The process, the delay, the waiting helps us to build our faith. Neal A. Maxwell said "Faith in God includes faith in God's timing. Believe that He's grouping resources, gathering people & grooming you for what He's about to do. Trust His timing & His plan even when it's hard!

Pray With Me
Lord of Lord and King of Kings, thank you God, our Father for being right on time when we need you. We do not always see it but your timing is truly perfect. Show us that in due season, we will see things change. We will see our prayers answered. For it is written, the prayers of the righteous avails much. Help us to have patience. Teach us to patiently wait on you, knowing that you are faithful and just. And even when we get impatient, Lord please calm our minds and remove any anxiety. You told us to be anxious for absolutely nothing, so help us to lean on you and talk to you to remove any anxiety as we wait on you to do what you have promised us. Remind us that you are not a man, that you should lie. Strengthen our hearts and minds to stay focused on you and not the situation. Strengthen us to keep our eyes on you so that we can see our circumstances, our delays, and our waiting seasons through spiritual eyes. Help us to focus on you and you alone. Help us to know that a delay is not a denial when you are involved. Help us to know that you

are sovereign. You are in control. Your divine timing is always just that, divine and right on time. In the name of Jesus, we pray. Amen.

Chapter 3

BIG BATTLES

I'VE LEARNED THAT THERE IS A RESILIENCE that comes with beating adversity, conquering battles, defeating obstacles; overcoming situations that you know only God could have given you victory over. In his sovereignty, he helped you be victorious even when it didn't look like it or it didn't seem like it. I like to think that God blessed me with a bounce back like no other. I was determined. It could only get better. After setback after setback, I was still standing. I was not going to quit. *This was not like therapy.* Quitting was not an option. I didn't need others to tell me not to quit. I knew that God was pushing me. He made me resilient. I was ready to go back to high school.

    I had full mobility in my left arm. My hair was short but at least I had some hair again. My neck brace was finally off and school was starting soon. I missed the last month of my tenth grade year so this was going to be great. The outpour of students, my peers, my friends that came to visit me in the hospital and at my house was unbelievable. *I did find out that there was a rumor about me that spread to multiple high schools in my hometown. The rumor was that I died. Some of the kids probably came to see for themselves if I was alive for real. They probably just wanted to lay eyes on me. If I read that news article about a teen being plucked out of a sunken car, I wouldn't have believed I survived either. Shoot, it happened to me and sometimes I still didn't believe it.* Regardless of why they came, they did and I'm forever grateful for every visit, every call, and every card.

I'll never forget walking up the back steps of my high school and opening those doors. I felt great. I felt normal. I defeated all these odds and I was back to being a sixteen year old student. I was an honor student and I always loved school. I loved my teachers. It was my happy place. *I can finally admit to all of that without feeling lame.* That year was no different except that I had to make up some classes but I did it with ease. By God's grace I was thriving. I was still an honor student. Each year got better and better. The time came when I was graduating from high school. Might I add that I was graduating with my expected graduating class! *Shout out to Class of 1998!* That was a big deal. And to think just a couple of years earlier, my mom was told that I may not live and if I did, I may have brain damage or be paralyzed from my neck down. *No signs of brain damage for me. I couldn't use that excuse even if I wanted to.* Life was good and graduation was the first step to the changes I wanted to see in my life.

After graduation, I was on a mission. Because I grew up with a single mother who graduated from high school and never had an opportunity to go to college that made me want so much more for my life. I didn't want to be a housekeeper like my mom and clean people's houses, hotel rooms and buildings. I didn't even want to clean my own house. I had dreams of hiring somebody like my mom to clean for me. *I wouldn't even mind hiring my actual mom to clean for me.* Now, don't get me wrong, there is absolutely nothing wrong with being a housekeeper. I had a cleaning business and there were plenty of times when I had to clean because no one else showed up to work. *I guess they didn't like cleaning either.*

I fully appreciate all housekeepers because it takes a lot to clean up after people. My mom had a God-given gift for cleaning. She excelled at it. You better believe that if my mom stepped in your house to clean, it was going to be immaculate when she finished. My mom always worked hard. I love and appreciate her. I'm grateful for every sacrifice she made for me and my brothers. Her struggles made me push. To be completely honest, her struggles made me never want to be anything like her. I've fought all my life to be the complete opposite of her.

When I was younger, I didn't like what my mom did for a living so I ended up stretching the truth. Have you ever stretched the truth about something? *And when I say "stretched the truth", I really mean lied.* In all transparency, I started lying at an early age, elementary school age. Such a strange thing to actually admit to, but it's true. I lied so much about my mom's career that even I started believing it. *I really hope you aren't judging me, but if you are, put down those stones. I have repented and turned from those ways. We all have fallen short. Maybe not as much as me or as early as I started but fallen short is fallen short.*

In fourth grade, I transferred schools in the middle of the school year. I didn't know these kids so I had a full blown lie that I told when kids asked me what my mom did for a living. *It was really none of their business but oh well.* I was already getting picked on because I was different. Several of the students picked on me because of how I dressed and how I talked. Get this, I was made fun of because I was smart and got along with my teachers. *Now, who's laughing!* Most of those people became my friends. In fact, in sixth grade I was voted Student Council President. *Just a humble little plug about my early leadership skills and popularity!* God turned that thing all the way around. I definitely didn't see any of that coming.

Because I was already getting joked on, I didn't want to give those kids more ammunition to use. My mom being a housekeeper was something that I knew they would rag on me about. So what lie did I tell? I told them my mom was a teacher. Thank God they never asked at what school. I don't know how deep I could've gone with this make-believe career that I gave my mom. The truth is that I was ashamed that my mom was a housekeeper. I was determined to never be a housekeeper. I wanted to go to the exact opposite end of the spectrum to be nothing like my mom. I had to go to college. My mom was not one of those parents that even talked to me about college at all. I guess because she didn't know anything about it.

My friend's parents on the other hand, not only talked about college, but forced them to apply to multiple schools. Well, for me I thank God for my village. I thank God for my godmother and godsister. My godmother was a professor at a local university so what my mom lacked in telling me, my godmother made sure to tell me. Because of my godmother, I knew I was going to go to college. I had friends that were already attending different universities and colleges. I had to figure out where to apply. The thing is that I couldn't afford to apply to several colleges. I couldn't afford college at all. Not to mention that my GPA was brought down because I didn't have grades for the last grading period of my sophomore year in high school. I missed ten days out of school and my mom didn't go to court to appeal the decision. I'm pretty sure that she was too busy being concerned about me in the hospital. I'm not even sure she knew about that rule. I should've known better and fought that. *Or maybe my mom should've*. Once again my traumatic car accident was shaping my life.

I ended up applying to a university where some of my friends already attended. I knew the chances were slim but if you never take the shot, you never have a chance of making it. One day the university's admission's office called me. *I didn't even know they made phone calls to talk about admission. And to think, I was waiting for a letter.* Well, since my transcript showed me as an honor student for all grading periods except for that last grading period in tenth grade, they wanted to discuss what happened. I told the really nice admission's lady all about my car accident and all that I had been through. I laid it on thick. By the end of the conversation she told me that they would be happy for me to attend the university. Me, myself and I along with my C average were headed to college.

I can truly say that I was disappointed that I had been an honor roll student all my life and would be entering college with barely an average GPA. I was entering college on academic probation. Who would have ever seen that coming? An honor student since kindergarten entered college on academic probation. It's amazing how you can work hard all your life and one incident or in my case, an accident can change everything. Have you ever unexpectedly experienced something in your life that changed your circumstances? Things happened that I never planned. Battles and challenges that I never thought I would be up against.

After being the MVP of surviving, I felt like I could take on anything. God had shown me that He was with me. I felt prepared for any opposition. But then my freshman year of college happened. My freshman year of college was the most academically challenging time of my entire educational career. When I say academically challenging, I mean I went from being an honor student since kindergarten to not being able to make an A to save my life. I'm a pretty strong person but my first semester of my freshman year tried to break me. After I entered the university on academic warning because of my C average, I just knew that when I got there I was going to turn that all around. Well, a lot of challenges came when I moved from home without any money or support. I didn't have any money at all. *I was broke, broke.* I didn't have any help and I was really struggling.

My mom basically packed up a turquoise trunk filled with all my clothes. She gave me what she could. She made sure I would be neat and clean. My mom literally washed, ironed and folded all my clothes. *If only she knew that was the last time they were going to be ironed.* I was dropped off at school to fend for myself. I was one of the first students on campus and definitely in my dorm. It was an older dorm. They called it the old teacher's dorm. It didn't matter what they called it. I was excited to actually have a place to stay. I was excited to attend the university.

One of the main things that people heading to college think about is roommates. I didn't think about who was going to be my roommate. I only thought about money. Forget about who was going to be my roommate. I was thinking about how I was going to pay for college. I didn't care who was in the room as long as I was in a room. I couldn't afford to have a private room so I knew that the chance of me having a dorm room to myself was slim to none. I was blessed though because no one else was assigned to my room. Look at God showing up and showing out again.

Freshman year was looking up. Well, it looked down after about a month or so after school started. *What were the odds that I wouldn't have a roommate? Yeah, slim to none was right.* A young lady from a city in Southern Alabama moved into my room. *Yes, I said my room. I was there first.* She seemed nice enough. We had so much in common if so much meant: we were both black young ladies attending a predominantly white university and we were both from the great state of Alabama.

It turned out that was all we had in common and that wasn't enough. She was a little different in the most awkward way. The way she dressed. The way she did or didn't do her hair. The way she talked. She had a peculiar personality. She made me uncomfortable at times. You could tell she was really, really smart. She was just awkward on another level. I did not realize it then but now I know that she was just socially awkward. *I definitely was not judging her even though it seems like it. I'm just stating facts.* This stuff was obvious to anyone that met her.

I did not know why God would send her to be my roommate. I began to understand though. Despite how peculiar and socially awkward I thought she was, she was good to me. God truly used her to be a blessing to me. Let's remember that I came to school with no money and no help. I applied for student loans and work study, but I hadn't heard back. Until I started working, I had to pinch off what I had, which was next to nothing. My new roommate was so nice that she would share everything. She would make sure that I ate. When she went to the grocery store she would get enough for both of us. Our room was blessed. *Yes, it officially changed from my room to our room.* With all the good though, there came some bad. I will never forget the day that the blessing turned into a lesson. I'll never forget the day that I questioned whether this roommate came from God or Satan.

Let it be known that I am really friendly. When I say friendly, remember that I'm that overly friendly person that talks to strangers in the elevator. *I can't help that a lot of people describe me as the person who doesn't meet a stranger at all.* So obviously I became friends with several of the girls in my dorm. I became really cool with one of the girls down the hallway. She came to our room to visit sometimes. This particular day that my friend came by, my roommate was "on one", which means she was just snippy. My new friend from down the hallway started talking to my roommate about something and a debate began. I was out of it. I wasn't even listening. I didn't even care. I stayed completely out of it. I was neutral. In fact, I didn't even know what they were talking about and neither did I want to know.

My friend ended up leaving because they had a disagreement. To this day I still don't know what the conversation was all about. I'll tell you what I do know. I will tell you what I will never forget. I remember my roommate came up to me and told me that I was supposed to be on her side because she shared her food with me. The moment that it came out of her mouth I could have punched her in her throat. *I am not a proponent of fighting. Well, not anymore!* God held me. She better be happy that God held me. He held me physically and I didn't touch her. He did not hold my mouth though. This was one of those freewill moments where the flesh was weak. I went off on her. Just imagine when Jesus got upset with the tax collectors and threw the table over. I felt myself getting hot. I was in her face and I let her have it. My word choice was not biblical. I did not pray about it. I did not remember anything I learned in church. I just went clean off. I definitely did not sound like the sweet, church going, miracle child who was graced with a second chance at life.

How dare she say that to me? I never asked her for anything. I was raised by a prideful woman who didn't ask anybody for anything. I was raised to not ask people for anything. How dare she offer and then throw it up in my face at her convenience! I went off on her and then I left the room which seemed like the right thing to do. To just walk away seemed like the best thing to do in that situation. I walked away but I slammed the door so hard that our Resident Assistant and everybody on the floor heard it. What happened next was pretty bad.

My roommate complained to our Resident Assistant. She said she was fearful of me. The girl said she was fearful for her life. *Really! And I thought I was a drama queen.* We had to have a meeting to discuss our living situation. I'll never forget being in that meeting with her and our Resident Assistant. In front of the Resident Assistant, I told her that if I wanted to do something to her, I would've done it already. *Yes, I said it with a smile on my face. Obviously she didn't know who she was dealing with.* My Resident Assistant calmly and politely said that one of us had to move out of the room. I should've seen that coming. How dare this girl come and create drama in my room! *Yes, it's back to being my room since she completely tripped out on me.* They barely let me into this university. I just wanted to go to class and stay off the radar. I did the best thing I knew to do. I decided to be the bigger and better person.

Yes, she had some issues but so did I. The reality was that my issues were not going to get any better around her. If this was a battle that God was using to show me something, I could not see it at all. The fight was over. Honestly, the fight should have never started. I should have ignored her. *Tell me why didn't I ignore her?* Getting extremely offended and not walking away calmly cost me my room. I was in the wrong and I knew it. I told my Resident Assistant that I would move out. I was used to moving anyway. That was the story of my life.

Have you ever been in the wrong and God still made a way for you in your own mess? I can raise my hand for sure. I did not see what was coming next. The process for moving me out and moving me into a new room ended up being easy. God not only made the process easy but He moved me from the old, rundown dorm to the upperclassman dorm. God showed me His divine favor. *The favor of God was on my life and on my old roommate whether she knew it or not.*

I didn't feel good about basically getting kicked out of my room but I did feel good that I stood up for myself. No, I didn't have to act like a fool on the girl but I felt good that I didn't allow my roommate to make me feel less than. I felt good that I didn't punch the girl in her throat. I felt good that I had grown some. I was proud of myself for walking away when I did. Obviously it could've been sooner but I was proud of myself for practicing some form of self-control. God intervened on my behalf. He was making a way for me. I definitely needed "easy" and "better" because it was closing in on the end of the semester. Finals were swiftly approaching.

They gave me a list of five young ladies whose rooms were open for consolidation. Since these girls had not paid for private dorm rooms, I could be moved into any of their rooms. It was the same way they moved my old roommate in on me. The only thing that was different with this situation was that as a courtesy, I called each one of the young ladies to introduce myself and then I was able to choose one. I chose a young lady who seemed so sweet and excited to have me as a roommate. Also an added bonus was that she was in a sorority, so I assumed she would not be in the room very often.

She was eager for me to move in. *Is there such a thing as being too eager to have a roommate? That should've been a red flag for me.* We had never met face to face but I liked her from our phone conversation. She was a Northerner. I knew this would be interesting. We were the complete opposite of each other. After my last roommate situation, I needed to do something different. She only knew my name and what we discussed on the phone.

Move-in day came quickly. When I was moving in, she wasn't there but the Resident Assistants and two of my friends were with me. I was moving in and my new roommate, who was so thrilled that I would be rooming with her, walked in and flipped out. It got worse and worse as she cried and yelled. She said that I couldn't stay there. The young lady actually said and I quote, "She can't stay here. If she does, I'm going to make her life a living hell." *Oh how quickly these roommates could turn on me. I once again needed God to intervene for me with yet another unstable roommate.*

The Resident Assistants explained to the new, spoiled, unstable roommate that her room was open for consolidation so it was not up to her for me to move in. They politely informed her that they had the authority to move anyone in the room. They told her that it was a courtesy that I spoke with her before moving in. Whether she agreed to me moving in or not, the room was not private and was open for consolidation.

Well, she was not having it. The poor girl was in tears. She said that she would pay to have a private room. I was looking and really just floored by this whole scene. *Was I being pranked? I didn't see any cameras. There definitely should have been some cameras somewhere the way she was acting. She was carrying on like a fool.* She said that her family had been at the university for five generations. She said she was going to call her mom who knew the president of the university. It was just a whole show. *And I thought I was dramatic!*

Everyone in the room was dumbfounded. My friends and I were like "this crazy girl". Of course, my extremely outspoken friend said "this white girl is tripping out because you're black". It finally sat in. She thought Elizabeth Williams was a white girl. I've been teased most of my life because of how I talk. Some of my black friends always told me I sounded like a white girl. They also said that I acted like a white girl too. *To this day, I don't know how someone can act or sound like a race. Was this part of the reason that my friends took my black card that same year because I hadn't seen Boyz N The Hood? No judgment. Plus, I've seen it now.*

Well, after a whole drama-filled show that the young lady put on, I finished moving in and stayed in the room for about a week, if that. She did indeed call her mom. Her mom did indeed make some calls. My new roommate and I had a meeting with the Director of Housing. He politely told me that since my lovely roommate, *you know the one, who cussed me out and had a meltdown when she saw me,* had applied for housing first that she would be staying in her room. The end result of that meeting was that I would have to move out of her room. He told me that they would find me a new room as soon as possible. This happened to me right when finals were coming up. I ended up sleeping in my friend's dorm suite most of the time. No surprise that I ended up failing most of my finals, especially math, which I wasn't doing well in before I was homeless.

My first semester of college was almost my last semester of college. One of the friends with me the day that I moved into my short-term room told her friend back home about what happened to me. They told me that the local newspaper wanted to interview me and do a story. I passed on it. I didn't want to cause any trouble. The fact was that the young lady came from a family with money. I didn't. She came from a family with privilege. I didn't. Her family had attended that university for five generations. Mine hadn't. The reality for me was that just some decades ago, no one that looked like me could even attend that university.

I was an eighteen year old college student who had no money, who wanted to go to school, keep my head down and become the first person from my family to graduate from college. Do I regret not fighting it? To be honest, as I've learned more about injustice, diversity, equity, and inclusion, my answer is a resounding *YES*. What happened to me wasn't right but I serve a God who is bigger than injustice.

Over the years, there have been many battles that God has fought for me. He will win the battle. In fact, I felt like these battles were the Lords. *Well not the one where I went off on the roommate and almost fought her, but the other one.* I've seen Him work and fight for me as weapons formed but could not prosper against me. God never said they wouldn't form. He said they would not prosper. Challenges with horrible roommates, being homeless and almost getting kicked out of college on multiple occasions had only made me stronger. I knew that BIG battles would help me to stand still and be victorious.

> For the Lord your God is he that goeth with you, to fight for you against your enemies, to save you.
> ~Deuteronomy 20:4 KJV

Do Me A Favor
Think about a time when you felt like the battles of life were weighing you down. When the battles of life close in around you and you feel surrounded, where do you turn? Do you turn to God? How do you let God fight your battles? Know that he will win. The reality is that he has already won which means that we have won. When Christ died for us, he rose with all power and that same power is in us. Are you in a battle that you're not even supposed to be fighting? Learn to seek God to find out if this is a battle that you should even be engaged in. I've learned that sometimes, God just wants us to be still and know that he is God. Learn to give your battles to him. Every challenge comes for us to grow in him. He allows some things to happen and it's alright. He won't let you be defeated. You're a child of the one and only living God. You are victorious.

Pray With Me
Father God, thank you for fighting our battles. Reassure us that the battle is not ours but it belongs to you. You have the victory in every situation. Help us to let go and let God. Help us to release our challenges and difficulties to you. Father, even when things are being done to us that don't seem fair, help us to know that you're going to bat for us. We are your children and you have promised us that you will never leave us or forsake us. We have the victory because

we believe that you are our heavenly Father. You told us that no weapon formed against us will prosper and we, by faith, believe that even when we see things forming, we know that it will not prosper. Father God, you are on our side. You have indeed blessed us and kept us. Since we're alive, it means that you're still fighting on our behalf. Thank you for fighting in the past, thank you for fighting now, thank you in advance for fighting every battle for us that we may face in the future. In the name of Jesus, we pray. Amen.

Chapter 4

BIG WISDOM

After dealing with one battle after the next and making it through, I was so thankful for God's grace on my life. I knew His grace was sufficient. If God's grace wasn't sufficient, I would not have made it to my sophomore/junior year of college. *Judgment free zone needed because the years started running together after failing, dropping and repeating classes.* It seemed as if I went through all the bad to get to this great place. I finally lived in a nice modern apartment. I was stable. My roommate's didn't show any signs of being unstable. *We know how that goes though.* I was working hard at school and on my job at a television station. Yes, I had a real job off campus, an adult job with adult hours. No more little work study for me. *Shame on me! It sure wasn't little when I needed it.* I would be in class all day and then go to work at the news station from 4 p.m. until 12 a.m. *Let me just tell you that getting off at midnight was no fun.* I was a different kind of college student. I had no choice but to be. I was the only student that I knew of who had a full class load and worked forty hours a week. I didn't party as much as I used to. *I mean who had the time for that.*

One day though, this older friend of mine was having a small party at his house and he invited me. *When I say older, I mean like* older than me. When I say friend, I mean like a brother from another mother. I asked one of my friends from class if she wanted to go. It didn't take much to convince her to go to a party. I didn't think twice about the fact that I had to work that night. Nowhere in my mind did I think about the fact that I didn't get off of work until midnight. I didn't think about the fact that I had been in class all day and worked all night. Nowhere in my mind did I think about the fact that I was going to be dirt tired. I was really tired, but I told my friend I was going to make it to his party. I made the mistake of inviting my friend, so I had to go. I was obviously going to a party on a weekday. *This was back in the days when I was a people pleaser and cared about disappointing people. I'm glad I've changed.*

    My friend met me at my apartment and left her car there. We headed over to the supposedly small party, which turned out to be a huge house party. There were a lot of people there. I didn't know anybody else other than my two friends. I only knew the friend who invited me and the one I brought with me. I wasn't really expecting to know anybody else. To be honest, I didn't want to even be there. I decided to make the most of it. My friend introduced me and my friend to one of his friends. He stood out like a sore thumb. He was a little different. From the moment that I was introduced to him, I thought he was a little strange, but he seemed nice. These people were older than me so it didn't matter if they were strange or not, nice or not. I would never see them again.

    The guy that stood out like a sore thumb was going on a beer run and he came to me to see if I wanted anything. I asked him if he didn't mind getting me some juice. Yes, believe it or not, I was the only person not drinking at the party. My friend was drinking. She was drinking enough for both of us so I was definitely the designated driver. When I asked for some juice, the guy started naming every juice he could think of. I guess he wanted to make sure that I knew the options and that he picked up what I wanted. I stopped him and told him some grape juice would be fine. He brought back a gallon of grape juice just for me. I tried to pay for it, but he refused my money. He really seemed like a nice and sweet guy. *Now that I'm thinking about it, I actually thought the same thing on two occasions with those roommates who landed me homeless and almost kicked out of school. I should have read that warning sign.*

About 3 a.m., I woke up after falling asleep in a chair. The party was still going on. My friend that came with me to the party was still playing cards. She was having a great time. *Good ole Spades!* I, on the other hand, was ready to go. My contacts were drying out and my eyes were burning. I was still dirt tired even after my brief nap. I told my friend about my contacts hoping that she would sympathize. She did. Finally we were about to leave. I couldn't find my friend that invited me to tell him that I was leaving, but at that point who cared. *I could thank him later for the invitation to the party that I shouldn't have even gone to.*

My friend and I made it back safely to my apartment. She headed to her car and a car pulled up to me. It was the nice guy from the party. He followed me home. Either this was a good thing or a bad thing, but as optimistic and somewhat naive as I was at times, I leaned towards good. He pulled up and called my name. *He had a good memory because I definitely didn't remember his name.* He told me that he wanted me to know that he followed me home. He continued to explain why he followed me which put me at ease. He told me that he followed me because he knew that I was tired and my contacts were bothering me. His explanation made sense to me. It was something that my friend that I couldn't find would have done to make sure that I made it home safely. He was pretty protective. I thanked the guy. I thought that was really nice of him. God's grace was indeed sufficient. God was once again watching over me and sending someone to look out for me.

Well, I know I'm going to be judged for the next thing that happened, but here we go. The guy asked me if he could use my bathroom. I told him sure. This was one of those moments in life where I didn't even think. *Now before you judge me too harshly, I had two other roommates and one of my roommates had a boyfriend that stayed over way too much. Also, there was a sheriff who lived directly above our apartment.* I wasn't afraid. I wasn't alarmed by anything. I really don't even remember thinking twice before saying sure. We had a friend in common and so I trusted him. He backed his car into a parking space and followed me into my apartment. I showed him to the bathroom and he went in to use it.

An important detail is that my friend had not left. She pulled her car up and came into my apartment while the guy was in the bathroom. She didn't want to leave when she saw the guy following me. She and I went into my room and were whispering about the guy. She asked me what was going on. I told her that the guy followed us and then asked to use my bathroom. The conversation stopped when I heard the toilet flush and then the water at the sink turned on and then turned off. I came out of my room but didn't see him. The light was dim up front. I went to my door and it was unlocked. My friend more than likely didn't lock it. The guy must have left and went home.

Now, this is where it gets unexplainable. The thing was that I didn't see the guy anywhere. Mind you it was dark up front. Hopefully you can envision this layout. The apartment had four bedrooms and two bathrooms. There were two bedrooms on each side and one bathroom on each side. The living room and kitchen were in the center of the apartment. Behind the small kitchen there was a closet/pantry with the washer and dryer in it. So imagine all the lights out except for the bathroom and my bedroom both which were around the corner from the shared living space. In other words, it was pretty dark in that kitchen area with no lights on.

For some reason, I looked at the kitchen and then opened the sliding pantry door which was cracked. The guy was standing up against the wall by the garbage can like some psycho. *What the heck? I know it sounds unbelievable but I honestly can't make this stuff up.* Now at this point anybody else would be freaking out but for some reason, I'm as calm as a cucumber. Instead of all the other things I was thinking to say, I say and I quote, "Oh, there you are." The guy came out and told me that I had a nice place. He walked to the door and left. How very bizarre that was. My friend came out of my room and we were tripping out. She was first tripping on me for letting a stranger into my apartment to use the bathroom. My defense will forever be that the guy looked innocent and he had just done a really nice thing by following us home to make sure we were safe. *Never mind, it still sounds bad to me now.* We live and we learn. My defense needs to be that I was twenty one years old and I was extremely naive. *Never mind, it still sounds bad to me.*

Well, the night was not over. Wait, this was actually early in the morning. My friend and I were sitting in the living room talking when we heard a loud car. We looked out the window and there was the guy's car. He drove this really loud old car. He was driving around my apartment complex parking lot. He left but then came back and turned his lights off. His car was on the side of the big dumpster in the parking lot. This was quickly turning into a Lifetime movie. We were looking right out the window at the guy sitting in his car. *You know how you crack the blinds open slightly so you can peek out? Yeah, we're doing that as if he could see us looking out in the dark.*

The guy ended up driving off again. When my friend first followed me in, she quickly moved her car from a parking space to the curb in front of my apartment. She decided to go back out and park into a parking space. She came back into my apartment after moving her car. Shortly after that, there was a knock at my door. Sure enough, it was the guy. I put the chain on the door and cracked it open. Guess what he wanted? Can you believe this guy had the audacity to ask me for our friend's number? You know he knew his number. They were friends way before I even met the other guy. It was obviously an excuse to come to my door. *I appreciate that there is no judgment for me actually answering the door. For the record, I had the chain latch across the door as he asked this stupid question.* After getting him away from my door, I thought this bizarre situation was over.

The next day was normal. It was a Friday. I went to class. I went to work. I came home. It turned out that it was just the beginning. This guy proceeded to come to my apartment in the middle of the night, after midnight, knocking on the door. My car hood was conveniently scratched by someone but no one knew anything about that. The last draw was when my roommate and I were coming back home from a party about 2 a.m. and guess who was walking away from our door. Yes, the stalker. I was speechless. *That very seldom happens.* I didn't know if I should be mad or feel sorry for him. He looked hopeless. He had his head down. I was the ratchet one but for some reason I didn't go off on him. My roommate/best friend on the other hand went off on him. She was yelling at him. She kept asking him what his problem was. He didn't say anything. She told him that if he didn't get away that she was going to call the police. He looked at me as he walked away. She told him not to look at me. It was just strange.

I had no idea why he was bothering me. I had no idea why he chose to interfere in my life. I didn't know him. I had only met him that one time. Talk about making a bad decision. I was nice to the wrong guy. This guy that looked like he wouldn't hurt a fly was indeed hurting me. I never knew when he would show up. I didn't know if he was following me. Surprisingly, I wasn't scared but I guess I should have been. I knew that I hadn't been through all I had been through to be fearful of some misunderstood guy. God was covering and keeping me.

My roommate/best friend and I talked about moving into another apartment. We talked to the apartment office manager. I really thought that this would solve the problem and I could go back to my normal life. I couldn't have seen what was coming next. My roommate/best friend and my other roommate had gotten together and told me that I had to move out. I had no choice but to move. It was two of them and one of me. Unlike me, they were scared. To make matters worse for me their parents were upset and scared for their safety. Not at the time but later, God opened my eyes and helped me to see myself in their shoes. If I had a daughter in college, away from home, I wouldn't have wanted her in that situation. I would have put myself out too. I had nowhere else to go so I had to drop my classes and go home. You may be asking why I didn't call the police. Well, my roommate called and the police confronted the guy. He told them that he was not harassing me and they dropped it. I was upset over that but once again, who was I to try and fight anything. I was a black college student claiming that a white adult male was harassing me. Nobody in that city wanted to hear that. Who had time or money to fight anything?

I wanted an education. I wanted to graduate from college. I already wasn't the best student but I was turning things around and then it all shattered again. I was so far behind. I was on academic probation again. The academic warnings from the university were quickly turning into "we're about to kick you out of school". My GPA wasn't even a 1.0 for that semester. *If you don't believe me, I will show you my transcript. It literally says 0.668. I'm not proud of it, but it is part of my testimony. It's part of God's grace.*

I had been an honor student all my life until college. The only "A+" I had seen since I started college was in HPL 120 Aerobics. *I was excited about working out when I first got to college so it took little effort to make a good grade in that extracurricular class.* I was yet in another situation that I didn't ask for. I was minding my own business at that get-together. I didn't ask to be stalked, harassed or whatever you want to call it. I did make the mistake of letting a stranger into my apartment. I can honestly say that I didn't use wisdom. In fact, that was one of the worst mistakes that I've made in my life. *And I have a long list of mistakes. It definitely made the Top 10.* I didn't want to get kicked out of school. What was I going to do? I did the only thing I knew to do. I prayed. I trusted God.

I was young, dumb and naive. I was messing up all over the place, but somehow God's grace found me right where I was. Isaiah 43:18-19 KJV says, "Remember ye not the former things, neither consider the things of old. Behold, I will do a new thing; now it shall spring forth; shall ye not know." I was determined to not sulk in the mistake I made. I was not considering the old. The enemy would have wanted nothing better than for me to feel bad about myself and the decision that I made, but I wasn't going to allow that. God wouldn't allow that. I couldn't go back and not let the guy use my bathroom. I couldn't go back and just not go to that dumb party that I didn't even want to go to. The past was the past. I had to take it as a lesson and use wisdom moving forward.

I had to figure out what my next step was. *No, wait! We, God and I, had to figure out our next step.* It turned out that getting kicked out/put out/thrown out on the streets was one of the best things that could have happened to me. I needed to regroup. I ended up going home. *As if I had any other choice, but to go home.* While I was at home, one of my friends connected me with one of his friends who needed a roommate. He knew her from church so I told him I didn't mind meeting her. *Why was I thinking that just because she went to church it was safe to meet her? I don't know. Had I not learned anything? I was acting as if I didn't just have a stalker. You can say it; here I go again, trusting strangers. When would I ever learn?* Well, I met her and she was actually really cool. I liked her. *Not that I was the best judge of character as you've read.*

I was prayerful about this one though and I stepped out on faith. I hadn't made any plans for where I was going to stay when I went back to school. I didn't know if I was going back to school. Not because I didn't want to but at this point I didn't know if I could. When I met this roommate, I truly felt like God was intervening to get me back at school. So, I told her I would be her roommate. She was acting like I did her a favor when the reality was that she did me a huge favor. Before meeting her, I didn't even know if I was going back to the university. She had no idea that God used her in my life from the point that we met. This roommate was an intricate part of what God wanted to bring in my life.

My roommate, *also known as my best roommate ever,* quickly turned from a stranger to a friend. Our personalities could not have been more different. We were on completely opposite ends of the spectrum. She didn't come across as friendly. She was more than likely a person that wouldn't speak to strangers in an elevator. She was extremely smart and driven. She was very mature. She was focused. I learned so much from her. And let me remind you that she was a freshman. We ended up becoming more like family. You know that your roommate actually likes you for real when you get invited to go home to spend the weekend with them and their family. This was the beginning of an interesting weekend.

My roommate and her family held true to my first impression of them. They were really nice people. Their southern hospitality made me feel so welcomed. It was good to see a family that looked like mine but didn't act like mine. *You know what I'm saying. They were civil and loving to one another.* It was good to see a black man in the role of a father and a husband. I had never seen that in my household.

My roommate was a positive role model for me especially academically. I studied more than I had studied my whole college career. It was no secret that I needed to bring my GPA up. I started excelling in class. I was in a stable environment and I felt good. There was no more moving around for me. As a result, my grades were better than they had ever been.

I still couldn't get it right with my math class, but God stepped in. Wisdom told me to take my math class at the local community college. That was one of the best academic decisions of my life. I finally understood my professor. I enjoyed my class even though I never liked math. I ended up not only passing but I made a 3.0 in math. *Who would've ever thought after all the failed and dropped classes that I would be saying that?* Community college was an answered prayer.

Another answered prayer was when my roommate and I landed jobs at a debt collection agency. Debt collection on returned checks was one of the highlights of my entire work career. It taught me customer service skills while creating jokes and laughs galore. I never thought that I would hear some of the things that I heard out of the mouths of some senior citizens who bounced checks at a dollar store. You can't imagine the numerous stories that I have. That job definitely added some excitement to my life and a little financial stability. Life was good. God was smiling on me. I just needed to continue seeking him for wisdom and direction.

A foolish mistake that I made landed me in the right place for what God wanted to do next in my life. Not using wisdom and being too friendly to a stranger took a lot from me but it added a lot as well. God used that favorite college roommate to literally change my life. One major connection happened when I was in college, but it all didn't come together until after I graduated. Something that I could have never seen coming happened to me. *You're going to be as shocked as I was.*

I am a very, very, very optimistic person. I always want to see the glass half full. I want the cup to overflow. I know that God gave me a kindhearted spirit and a unique optimism that allows me to choose to see the best in everybody. But honestly we live in a dark and fallen world. People will do anything. Some people have bad motives. I don't have to think the worst of everyone but I also have to be cautious. I know that people are capable of anything. I have to use wisdom and discernment. Godly wisdom to me means that I pray and listen to the Holy Spirit. Through everything, God's grace was truly sufficient. His grace made up for my lack of wisdom. *I know that the devil was mad about that one. Absolute failure in trying to take me out!* I took so much from that experience and I praised God throughout the situation. I learned that I needed BIG wisdom. I learned that BIG wisdom is available to me but I have to seek it and use it.

> See then that ye walk circumspectly, not as fools, but as wise, [16] redeeming the time, because the days are evil.
> ~Ephesians 5:15-16 KJV

> If any of you lack wisdom, let him ask of God, that giveth to all men liberally, and upbraideth not; and it shall be given him. ~James 1:5 KJV

Do Me A Favor

Ask yourself these questions: Have you ever done something that you consider a mistake or ever used bad judgment? Did you consult God before doing it? *If you've never made a mistake or used bad judgment, please email me so I can set up a meeting with the person claiming to be Jesus.* Nobody's perfect. I'm not saying that you didn't use wisdom and let a stranger into your apartment, but we all have done something that we're not proud of. Some type of mistake, error that cost us something. A decision that we made or didn't make caused us some grief. We literally have all sinned and fallen short of God's glory. God knew this so he sent Jesus. And knowing that we have Jesus Christ and the Holy Spirit, we need to use that help. We need to stop and ask for help. We need to use wisdom. Take a moment and think about whatever your mistake was. How different would it have turned out if you had consulted God first? That's wisdom. That's doing it God's way.

Pray With Me

Father God, thank you for your grace that covers our lives. Thank you for your wisdom and knowledge that you give us. Even when we do not understand your ways and we decide to do it our own way, you are faithful. Father you have given us everything that we need to do this life with and we thank you. In times when we don't know the answer, help us to slow down and seek you. Help us to seek you and obey you when your Holy Spirit is nudging us and giving us your answer. Thank you for blessing us even in the situations where we made a mistake or made a bad decision in judgment. If we didn't listen to you, please forgive us. We know that you have already forgiven us, Father. Thank you for releasing our guilt and shame. We thank you for allowing us to feel freedom knowing that because we have released it all to you that the enemy can no longer hold it over our heads to make us feel less than. Thank you that we are more than conquerors and we are equipped with your wisdom. You're a loving and good, good Father. We praise you. In the matchless and mighty name of Jesus, we pray. Amen.

Chapter 5

BIG PLANS

After all of the bad grades, drama and horrible roommates, I actually graduated from college. It might have taken a little longer than expected. *Wait, who am I kidding? After my first year of college, I knew I wouldn't graduate in four years. I could settle for five years. As if I had a choice.* Honestly, I was just happy to actually graduate from college. I didn't give up. God wouldn't let me give up. There was something in me that kept pushing me. There was something in me that made me keep coming back after everything the enemy was throwing at me. There was a resilience that kept me bouncing back. God had a plan for my life. There was obviously a purpose and a plan for me.

I was ready for the next chapter of life. I was ready for my official adulthood. I'll never forget sitting down at my godmother's computer and applying for jobs after my Post Graduation Plan crashed and burned. *I'm not being dramatic this time.* What exactly was my Post Graduation Plan? *I'm glad you asked.* My plan was to work at a law office back home as an office assistant. Any breaks that I had from school, I came home and you would find me at the law office working. I loved it. I wanted to be a lawyer until I found out how much it cost to go to law school and how long it took. *Quickly scratched that off the list!*

Even though my dreams of being a lawyer were non-existent, I still really enjoyed working at the law office during the summers and holidays. In spite of the office staff being small and stretched thin, they took their time out to talk to me about processes. I did more than just run errands. They taught me about legal documents and legal language. *Don't ask me anything now because I don't remember but at the time, I was on it!* The office manager at the law office told me that I was guaranteed a job there after I graduated. No, I hadn't prayed about it. I hadn't consulted God to see if this was the plan that he had for me. I just knew that this was the path for me.

Well they must've changed their mind. *Or God changed it for them.* They obviously didn't think it was the path for me when they gave the job to someone else. To be honest, it wasn't their fault. We had a little miscommunication from the person who was earning a degree in communication *(i.e. me). I know it's just sad, right.* They thought I was graduating in May. Due to a stalker and even before that, my poor start in my college career, I didn't graduate until that August. So as I sat at that computer with no law office job after graduation, I didn't have a plan. I only had prayer. *Yes, now I decided to lean and depend on Jesus. Remember, no judgment.* I was looking for jobs, which was a road I definitely did not think I would be on.

Job searching was no fun at all. *Especially when I had no idea that I was going to have to search for a job at all!* I decided that even though the door completely closed on my plans, there had to be a better plan. I just didn't know what the plan was. God was on my side and if one door closed another one was certainly going to open. With my degree in Communication and Information Sciences, the sky was the limit. God doesn't put limits on anything and I wasn't going to either. I was determined. *I was the miracle girl who had been trapped in a car that was submerged underwater for over ten minutes who had two broken bones in her neck and lived with no paralysis or brain damage.* I needed a job and I was going to get a job. I served a limitless God who could do the impossible. *Impossible is what it seemed like as I searched for a job…absolutely impossible!*

There were numerous job listings and I was an ideal candidate for most of them. *Well, at least I thought I was. I mean I would have hired me on the spot.* I was just looking for something entry-level even though I had what I thought was tons of experience for a new college graduate. Most days I was motivated but on the days that I wasn't I had the best boyfriend/best friend that encouraged me. I was learning more and more that God was always placing people around me to motivate and support me. I was going to find a job. I had to find a job.

One day, the perfect job came across the computer screen. *The job search website was indeed looking out for a sista!* There it was. The perfect job as a production assistant for a popular talk show was waiting for me. God heard my prayers and answered. I was already an experienced production assistant. My first job was a production assistant for a public broadcasting station in my hometown during a summer of college. *I really should've been taking classes in the summer to make up for those horrible grades but oh well.* My major in college was Telecommunication and Film (TCF). For one of my TCF classes, we had to put on a television show. I hosted and produced a show called Sports Today that aired on our campus channel. *Oh, you couldn't tell me anything!*

Yes, I wanted to be a producer. I had these big dreams of producing and hosting a television show. What made me even more qualified for the job was that I was a production assistant and master control operator for a news station. Yes, for two semesters, I was working hard at that television station. That was one of the best jobs I had in college. I was well on my way to achieving my goal of being a producer and talk show host. I was a production assistant for the newscast. I trained and then became a master control operator. This was the job where I had to be at work at 4 p.m. and I got off at midnight. *I wasn't kidding when I said I had to work 40 hours a week while taking a full load of classes. The struggle was real.*

Now let me just tell you that most of the time being a master control operator was the most boring job but it had its moments. What is a master control operator? *Well, I'm glad you asked.* My definition is a person that controls what you see on your television screen. I would play the commercial breaks and bring the shows back up. I could even make the screen go black, which I did several times just for fun. *It wasn't professional, but it also wasn't obvious because I didn't get fired.* This production assistant job at this popular television talk show was mine. I felt so sure of myself. I had a confidence like no other. I quickly applied. Well, it turned out that I needed more than my confidence, my firm work experience in college, and my prayers to work for this popular talk show. I was devastated that I didn't get the job. I was really devastated.

The host of the show was one of my role models. Growing up I wanted to host a talk show just like her. I could imagine myself working on her set. I imagined telling my talk show coworkers about my testimony and then one of them would tell her about me. Of course then she would want to meet me. I would tell her all about my traumatic life. She would then invite me to be a guest on her show. After my appearance on her show, I would get a book deal. *As you can see I had a lot riding on getting that entry level job.* Well, that was not God's plan. I was completely rejected, denied, but I did not have time to sulk in my disappointment. I was ambitious and if I wasn't going to be a production assistant at least I knew now more than ever that I wanted to work in television.

BIG PLANS

What's the next best thing after a very popular talk show? The next best thing was working for a local television station in my hometown. I applied for an account executive position at a local station that wasn't really local. *I was confused because the station was actually in another city but the office was in my hometown. Don't ask me y'all. I didn't understand.* Long and behold, I landed the job. Finally I was a working woman. God opened the door and I was walking straight through it. I graduated in August and landed a job in October. It seemed like a long time but in actuality it was only a couple of months. Don't tell me what God can't do. I will always tell you what He can do.

To be honest, I knew nothing about being an account executive. I remember sitting in the interview with the office manager and general manager hoping that they would go for my personality and charm. I sure didn't know anything about advertising sales, creating proposals or filming and writing commercials. I was eager to learn though. The word "executive" in my title made me feel important. *It was a different type of executive, but I took it as foreshadowing. A woman can dream, right?* I was going to learn to be the best account executive I could be. I was going to use my people skills to the best of my ability and believe that God would show me everything that I needed to know.

The job was a big blessing for me. At the time, I was living in my mom's one bedroom apartment. *We all know that wasn't going to fly for long.* My mom and I would get along for the most part, but we were just so different. There would always be some type of disconnect. There were so many unresolved issues that we never talked about. Those issues kept hunting me. When I didn't want to be at my mom's apartment, you could find me at my godmother's house. It seemed like God was always creating an escape route for me. He wouldn't let me be tempted or tested beyond what I could bear. Work was great most days. I loved my coworkers. We became friends. We helped each other with cold calls and producing commercial spots. We worked well together as a team. *I'll be completely honest and tell you that there were some challenging days when it came to our manager. I'm not sure how to even explain that without making people look bad, but I'll try.*

Let me first say that I was blessed with a nice manager. He was a little awkward, but I loved the way he would read his Bible at the office. He was just a nice guy. When I had an issue, he would take me in his office and take out his Bible. He would pick out a passage that fit whatever I was going through. I developed that relationship with my manager even though he could be difficult to work with at times. I knew I was being tested. I didn't quite understand it at the time, but I know now that I was being tested to see if I would stand strong. I was standing strong while my coworkers were all on the verge of quitting. The day that our manager made one of my coworkers cry was the last draw for her. *It wasn't the first time and she was a pretty tough young lady.*

It was no surprise to me when she ended up leaving the television station. We were about the same age and even though I wanted to leave as well, I couldn't take the risk. Even though she showed me that there were other options out there, I didn't want to take the risk. I saw the options, but I wasn't brave enough to go for them. I continued to stay in a toxic job situation. I needed my job. I was in my own apartment. I had grown folk's bills to pay. *We all know that I wasn't going back to Mommy Dearest place.* I would be alright where I was. I needed my paycheck. I was earning a commission check from my sales each month.

Something happened though that changed my tune really quickly. One day, the manager told us that our checks were being held. Well, all you had to do is mess with my money and I was not trying to be loyal and stand any ground. *I would withstand the drama, but what I wasn't going to do was be unpaid to deal with it!* I really did feel like this was the best job for me right out of college. I learned so much. All of this was past tense. After being there for a little over two years, I knew the season was up. I knew that God needed to open a new door. I knew that He was going to open a new door because an abundant life didn't look like "no paycheck and getting kicked out of my apartment." I couldn't have gone through all that I had gone through to not get wiser. I started being prayerful about God opening a new door. I was going to be still and know that He was God.

I was using everything that God was showing me to keep moving towards the plans that He had for me. *Moving forward in my mind, while staying on this job where they held my check that one time was a trying time. Shut, who knew when that one time would happen again!* Just because I had a little drama though, didn't mean that I couldn't see God in the midst of the situation. I had been through enough to know that I believed it was God that was directing. He was leading me. If He brought me to this job, there was a good reason. If He was keeping me at this job, there was a good reason. *I had to find those reasons and hold on to them because my optimism was quickly going out the door. I was getting beyond weary during my well doing.*

One of the reasons God brought me to this job was my clients. I loved my clients. Being able to work with small business owners, especially the black owned small businesses, was the highlight of my time at that job. To this day, I am still friends with some of the people that I met during that season of my life. I have been able to call on them and vice versa. I built strong relationships through that job. The other reason was my great coworkers. They may have left the job but we stayed in touch. We would go to lunch and still talk on the phone. One day, I received a call from my old coworker and she told me that there was a new position available doing what she did. She told me that she told her boss all about me and she needed me to send over my resume. She told me that they were ready to hire me on the spot as a donor recruiter. She didn't even give me time to take it all in. *I didn't know what a donor recruiter did, but let's remember that I also didn't know anything about being an account executive and I rocked with that for years.*

    I prayed and God answered. He opened the door. There was no way I wasn't going to walk through that door. There was absolutely no way that I wasn't taking that job. *My old coworker was happy and I bet she was getting her check on time.* God was paving the way. I must say that I enjoyed being a donor recruiter, but once again management had to mess things up. The company was raising our monthly goals. There was only so much I could do to convince people to donate blood. *Oh yeah! My bad, I was a blood donor recruiter.* I wasn't on that job for a year before I was blessed with a new opportunity.

    One day I was working a blood drive and I was honestly being my friendly, cheerful self when a lady told me that I needed to work for the organization that she worked for. Mind you that I didn't know this lady. I didn't know the lady that was seconding the motion that I should work for the organization. There I was at a blood drive on the bloodmobile doing my job and God sent this woman to offer me a job. She wrote the position and the manager's name on the back of her card. She told me to give him a call. I knew that I needed a new job. They were raising the goals and I couldn't keep trying to get blood out of a turnip.

    Get this; the lady was an executive at the organization. I read her card and I was floored. She saw something in me and thought that I should work for them. Well, my excitement turned to disappointment when I saw the name of the position. It said Marketing

Assistant. *Ha! What! I was in the working force for almost three years and she wanted me to be somebody's assistant.*

I just knew that I wasn't going to call that number about that job. The Holy Spirit wouldn't let me go about it though. I prayed about the position and before the week was up, I called him. I ended up having a great interview. I was hired. I humbled myself and I took a pay cut. Let me tell you though that less than a year later, I was promoted. God elevated me just like that. I couldn't have imagined the plans that He had in store for me. Sixteen years later, I am still with the organization and I've been promoted during that time. I've been blessed to do so many things working for a faith-based organization. Are you ready for this? I work for the same hospital system where I was unconscious in the ICU after my car accident when I was sixteen years old. God made a full circle. I think about how He placed me at a local television station where I met a coworker who after leaving the station called me to work with her and then I met an executive who worked for the hospital where my life was saved. *It gives me chill bumps.*

I couldn't have planned any of that. I couldn't have known that one thing would lead to the other. I truly believed that God was orchestrating people and things in my life for His plan and purpose. God has a purpose for everything under the sun. When He is involved there are no accidents or coincidences in my book. *No pun intended.* I hadn't gone through all that I had been through for God to not want to use it all for His purpose and His plan. Every disappointment, every bad break, every struggle was for His purpose and plan. He was lining up things on my behalf. He was placing the right people in my path that would get me to the next step, to the next thing that He wanted to do in my life. God's plans are always better than my plans. And boy, were there BIG plans in store.

Commit thy works unto the LORD, and thy thoughts shall be established. ~Proverbs 16:3 KJV

The steps of a good man are ordered by the Lord: and he delighteth in his way. ~Psalm 37:23 KJV

For my thoughts are not your thoughts, neither are your ways my ways, saith the Lord. ⁹ For as the heavens are higher than the earth, so are my ways higher than your ways, and my thoughts than your thoughts. ~Isaiah 55:8-9 KJV

Do Me A Favor

Think about a time in your life where you created and executed a plan to achieve a goal. Did your plan work out? Did you accomplish the goal? If not, why do you think it didn't work out? How did you feel when it didn't work out? If your plan succeeded, why do you think it did? Did you involve God in your plan? Did you consult Him to find out if your plan was aligned with His? Are you a planner by nature? I ask that because sometimes we want to control things. Some of us are planners by nature, so we can come up with the plan and organize everything. *Okay, well not you but me. I said some of us.* The problem comes in when we don't consult God and we want to handle it all on our own. Begin to go to the source. Remember that His plans are better than yours. Let Him get in the driving seat.

One more question. Do you dream big? God has given us dreams, visions and goals. He wants us to know that He has a plan for us. His plan is bigger and better than anything that we can imagine. We have to learn to step out on faith and know that He is right with us. He's leading and directing us. He is guiding us to an expected end. He's gone before us and He knows what is best for us. Imagine yourself on a set of stairs. It is completely dark. It is so dark that you can't see your hand in front of your face. A spotlight comes on and it is on your feet. The spotlight moves to the next step. You can only step where the spotlight is because you can't see anything else. That's exactly what God does sometimes. He does not show you the entire way. He gives you just enough light for the step you're on and then He moves that light to the next step. He is guiding you and you don't need to step anywhere else except for where He wants you to go, where He needs you to go. He knew you before you were formed in your mother's womb. He knows the plan that He has for you. Trust Him to guide you. Trust Him as He gives you just enough light for the plan that he has for you.

Pray With Me

Father God, Jehovah Jireh, our Provider, we thank you for blessing us with dreams, goals, plans and visions. We are so grateful that you want the very best for us. You have placed desires in our hearts. We long to fulfill all that you have set out for us to do. We are so grateful that you know every need that we have before we even know it and you have already met them. Father God, we thank you for orchestrating the way that you do. You're working behind the scenes on our behalf. You have placed people in our lives for reasons, seasons and lifetimes. We thank you for creating connections in our lives. Help us to recognize where each person on our path fits in your plans for us. Help us to know that you have a purpose for every connection. Father God, help us to seek you more daily that you may reveal to us the plans that you have for us. We know that if we do our part that you will indeed do your part. We know that according to your word in Jeremiah 29:11, that your plans are for good, plans to prosper and not to harm us, to give us a hope and a future. We thank you that we have reassurance that your plans are for good. No matter what happens, we can stand strong in our faith knowing that you have a plan for each of us. We thank you that you are indeed ordering our steps to go the way in which you have planned for us. In the name of Jesus, we pray. Amen.

Chapter 6
BIG LOVE

WHEN I THINK ABOUT ALL THE CONNECTING, orchestrating and planning that God has done in my life, I think about all the people He's brought in my life. I think about all the people He connected me to in order to work in my life to connect me to something else or someone else. One of the biggest connections of my life was when I met my favorite roommate in college. *You remember her. She's the one after the stalker. Let's not pretend that I had a lot of great roommates. Well, at least not in my book. No pun intended.*

My whole life changed when I ended up spending the weekend with my roommate and her family back in her hometown. I met her family when we were moving in and they seemed really nice. I stereotyped her dad as a former football player in college because he was a huge guy. He stood tall. You could tell he was an athlete back in the day. I had no doubt that he played offensive lineman or defensive tackle on somebody's football team. *I'm from the South. I know football. It's all about the SEC.* There was something about her dad. He was a big guy with a deep voice. He looked extremely intimidating to me. *Let me tell you that I never wanted to make him mad.* Looks are deceiving. *Assumptions are, well you know what they say about assuming.* He was the nicest man ever. He was a gentle giant. I loved his relationship with his family. I loved the way he treated his wife. I loved the way he treated his daughter and son. His father/daughter relationship made me smile. It even made me a little envious.

I was spot on with my assumptions. He was indeed a football player. He started talking to me about his college days, back in the day. Her dad was just making conversation. There's nothing wrong with reminiscing. I was going to humor him. My roommate's dad took out his old college yearbook and flipped through the pages looking for someone. He pointed out a picture of a guy and said, "Well, you look like my old football buddy from college." *There is something about older people in small towns, they know everybody or at least they think they do.* He asked about my parents. *Actually, he asked, and I quote, "Who are your folks?"* The sad thing was that after being alive for twenty-one years, I didn't even know my dad's name. It actually was really embarrassing.

I told him that my dad died when I was really young and that I never knew him. He told me that he was sorry. The conversation took a turn when I told him that when I was growing up someone told me that he died of cancer but I don't know anything else. *I don't even remember who told me that.* Why did I tell him that? Somehow that sparked more interest. Why couldn't I have just let it go with telling him that my dad died? Instead I had to add on the part about someone telling me that he died of cancer. I didn't have any other information. How could I have never asked my mom anything? Why was it a conversation that I was dreading to even begin having with my mom? The truth was that I somewhat favored the guy that he showed me in that yearbook. I told her dad that maybe he could be related to me. He told me maybe and we left it alone.

Let's fast forward to a couple of years after that great conversation with her dad. *You know the embarrassing one where I knew nothing about my family tree.* As you know, I finally, finally graduated from college in August of 2003. I left the best roommate I've ever had. I went back to my hometown and life went on. I do this thing every once in a while where I change number. *Don't judge me.* I literally changed phone numbers all the time. The really sad thing is that I often forget to let people know that I changed my phone number. It's not until I randomly bump into people that they get the new number. There are plenty of people that I've simply lost touch with. I was determined that my best roommate that I've ever had was not going to be one of those people.

I didn't think of my old roommate until that Thanksgiving holiday. About three months passed and I hadn't reached out to her. I know God placed her on my heart and mind. For some reason, I called to check on her and her family. When she answered, she told me that she wanted to get in touch with me because her dad saw my dad at the racetrack. *No, you aren't missing anything. Yes, just a paragraph ago, I told them that my dad died of cancer. No, I never said anything otherwise. No, we hadn't talked about it anymore after that.* But yet, I am talking to my old roommate who tells me that my dad wants me to call him. I know it sounds unbelievable but I can't make this stuff up.

In true Liz style, I took the number and called him. *You know me and strangers, plus my curiosity was a recipe for disaster.* Yes, I called a random guy who said he was my dad. *You know, the same dad that died of cancer when I was a little girl.* Get this though, when I called this random guy, he didn't even answer. His voicemail picked up. I obviously didn't want to leave a voicemail. What was I going to say? I'm the person that you think is your daughter? *No sir, that's okay.* I quickly hung up and thought God spared me from that foolishness. To my surprise, my phone rang. It was the random guy calling me back. *Caller ID will get you every time.* He asked if someone called his number. I told him exactly what I wasn't going to leave on the voicemail. I told him that my old roommate's dad saw him and they told me that he wanted me to call him. I told this man that they said that you said that you're my dad. He was excited that I called. I don't know any men out there that are just going around claiming kids. I don't know any men that just want to add another kid to their list. *I do know some that are trying to not claim their kids. I'm just saying.*

The conversation started and it wouldn't stop. It was two friendly, outgoing people talking to each other like we weren't complete strangers. *Lord, please help me.* The guy started telling me about my family. He was saying names of family members. He was saying street names that I heard family members bring up. He asked me what my mom told me about him. He asked me what my mom told me about them. I told him actually nothing. Then I paused to tell him exactly what I knew I had to tell him. I felt that it had to be said, so I said it. I told him that when I was a little girl someone told me that he died of cancer. His response actually was literally the way that I would have responded. He laughed and said something quick-witted. He made a whole joke out of it. We had a good conversation. What happened next even shocked me. I totally was not expecting what came next.

His excitement caused him to give me a proposition. I didn't even know this man and he was talking to me like he knew me. He told me that he was out of town but he was thinking about coming back to town that night. He said if I agreed to meet him, he would get on the road. You already know what my answer was. I was a somewhat naive twenty-three year old so I agreed to meet a stranger. I was so intrigued. I was so curious. I at least had enough sense to drag my cousin with me. At least I would not be alone to go meet "Daddy Dearest". I really didn't have to "drag" my sweet cousin who was only in town for the holidays. It did not take much convincing at all. She was equally as curious as I was. We planned to meet in a grocery store parking lot not far from where I was staying.

We actually drove down the same street where my accident happened seven years prior, to meet this man who said that he was my dad. *Let's remember that this is the deceased dad. I'm just reminding you.* There were times like these when I would really begin to wonder what exactly God was up to. We got to the parking lot and I realized that I told the man that I would be in a red Honda Civic but never asked what type of car he would be in. *The things you forget about when making a plan to meet up with a stranger at night. Once again, had I not learned anything?* Well, the man drove up and I knew it was him. We favored each other. What if this man was really my dad? I think from the moment I saw him, I was convinced that he was my father. I forgot all about what was told to me when I was younger. I don't know if it was just the thought of having a living father that got me all excited or not.

He told me that my grandmother was in town and he wanted me to follow him to where she was staying. You already know what I did. I followed this stranger to a neighborhood where his mom, my so-called grandmother, was staying. I trailed this man over to the Westside of town. True enough, I grew up over there and my aunt lived down the street but it really wasn't the brightest thing to do. Following this man, this stranger anywhere was not a bright thing to do. *Man, God has really covered me from some stuff. Grace upon grace.* We parked and went in the back door of this house. A lady who looked too young to be that man's mother looked at me and my cousin and asked which one of us was her granddaughter. She hugged me and my cousin. I knew I would like her. For a moment,

I wasn't thinking about if this guy was my father or not. I felt God smiling on me. This woman was extremely loving and kind. Her embrace was so warm. I felt like I belonged.

I grew up without grandparents. My mom's parents died when I was only four years old. My mom was twenty-nine years old when both of her parents died. I can't imagine not even being thirty years old and both of your parents are gone. To make matters worse, they died four months after each other. My mom's mother passed away and then her father passed away. My mom was so closed off that I never talked to her about my grandparents. Everything I learned about them was told to me by my favorite aunt and cousin. My grandparents lived through the stories that were shared with me. The stories were great, but now I had an opportunity to have a living grandmother who could tell me her stories. I wanted to know so much. Wow! What in the world was going on?

There were so many questions. How was this possible? *I believe that Jesus raised Lazarus from the dead but Jesus, my dad too. Let's not forget that he supposedly died of cancer.* Was this my dad for real? Was this amazing, happy, extroverted woman my grandma? Was this all true? Other questions quickly formed in my mind though. What am I going to say to my mom? Oh, wait, seriously, what am I going to say to my mom? How could I explain that I met some stranger who said that he's my dad? I've literally never talked to my mom about my dad ever. What would my mom say when I told her about this man who claimed to be my father? Recall the description that I previously gave you of my mom. It still held true. She was stern, introverted, prideful and not easy to talk to. *Hence, the reason that I was twenty-three years old and had never brought up my dad to her.*

Let's also remember that my mom's parents passed away four months after each other when she was twenty-nine years old. Let's remember that her mother passed away and then her father passed away four months later. That would be hard for anyone. I honestly thought she didn't talk about anyone that died because it was hard for her. Why would this not be the same case with my father? I honestly thought for as long as I can remember that my dad died of cancer. My so-called dad ended up telling me something that made me trust him. He told me that he knew I had a relationship with my mom and I didn't know him, so he didn't want to tell me anything that would hurt my relationship with my mom. He told me that I needed to talk to her. He said that he would wait until she told me what she wanted to tell me about him and them. I didn't know this guy, but I had some respect for him.

After my fun filled night with a man who claimed to be my dad, the next day came. I was not thinking this is the day that the Lord has made, I should rejoice in it. I was thinking "Lord, please keep me". Today was the day that I was supposed to confront my mom. *Wait, confront just sounds bad, especially talking about confronting my mama. Oh, no ma'am!* Let's simply just say that I was going to talk to my mom about this guy who says that he's my dad. I was a grown woman and afraid to talk to my mom. I was twenty-three years old and because my family didn't talk about personal things, I didn't know how to talk to my mom. I didn't know what to say. This guy gave me pointers on how to approach my mom and what to say. *He sounded like a professional. I think he'd been down this road a time or two.*

He told me to ask my mom if he knew him. When she responded yes, I was supposed to say "well he says that he's my dad". This was simple enough. My life had been full of complications but at this point, I was ready for anything. God was truly up to something this time. I was ready but not really. I went to my mom's apartment. I walked in and I'll never forget that she was standing in the kitchen.

It was a neutral and loving place to have this unbelievably awkward conversation. I told her that I wanted to talk to her. My mom was not a talker. I think just saying that made her nervous but she would never show it. Let's remember the previous description of her.

My mom and I never talked about life. She definitely would sit down and have a whole hour conversation about wrestling but anything other than that "nope". I just wanted to get this over with. I was just going to go by my new dad's script and say it word for word. I began with the question that would set the tone for me to just tell her that I met my dad. I cleared my throat and I asked my mom exactly what my so-called dad told me to ask her. I asked her if she knew the guy. My mom quickly and sternly responded by saying "No". *Hold up. What? This is not the way this conversation was supposed to go.*

Even if I was unsure about if this guy that I looked like was my father or not, I knew for sure that she at least knew him. The night before, he told me things about my family. He knew my mom's parents when they were living. He knew my aunts and uncles. He knew the places that we lived. He knew way too much to be someone that my mom didn't even know. Where do you even go from there? Was I supposed to continue with the script? My so-called dad didn't tell me what to do if she said no. I guess he wasn't banking on my mom flat out lying. Well I wasn't either. The only thing I could think to do was to say, he says he's my dad.

I didn't know what was coming next. She was in the kitchen. There were knives and cast iron pans all around. Anything could have been thrown at any moment. Lord, please let this be alright and we just move on from this. We couldn't do that though because my mom. The person who raised me, who made sacrifices for me, who did the best that she could do said something that changed my perception of her. My mom told me "that's my past". The words literally hurt. She didn't deny that he was my father. She didn't say anything else. Those three words hurt to the core. I don't know if it was because I felt like it was an omission about this guy being my father which means that my entire life I lived a lie. I don't know if it was because I felt like my mom just really didn't care. At that moment though, I stood there with an undeniable pain in my heart. I looked at my mom with tears running down my face and I told her that it may be her past but it's my present and my future. I turned and I left my mom's apartment.

I got in my car and called my dad. There was no more so-called dad. At that moment, I knew that he was indeed my dad. I told him what happened. He was a breath of fresh air. He talked to me like he knew me. He talked to me like he cared. He talked to me like he loved me. It didn't make everything that happened in the past right but in that moment it was what I needed. In that moment of confusion, hurt, pain and uncertainty, God knew what I needed. I needed a parent who possessed compassion. I needed something I had never had before.

This chapter of my life was just beginning. I had a living father. For years, I only had a heavenly father that I knew would always be with me. I wholeheartedly believe it was God who brought this man in my life. The road ahead was going to be rough. I had to adapt to having a father in my life. Not only did I have to adapt to having a father but I had four brothers and two sisters. *Was this a blessing from God or going to be something else that the enemy was going to use to try to distract me?* Seven kids with seven different women seemed like there was bound to be some drama. *No wonder my mom didn't want anything to do with him. Papa was for sure a rolling stone. No judgment though!* I honestly had a lot of brothers and sisters.

I'll never forget the first time I talked to my sisters on the phone. One of them asked me "where did you come from?" I told her that

I wasn't looking for him and that he found me. I knew that she was going to be a work of art. We're actually just alike. Our birthdays are ten days apart. We couldn't help but grow to become the best of friends. Now my other sister, who is the same age as my birthday-twin sister, was so nice to me when she met me. She may have talked behind my back or had the thoughts that my other sister said out loud. *Who knows!* We all became best friends. My sisters and I are really close. They are God sent. We have an undeniable love for each other. We're as thick as thieves. We have argued and made up. We've gone to bat for each other. We unconditionally love each other. It is as if I have known them all my life.

My relationship with my father on the other hand was pretty rocky for me. Don't get me wrong, I was happy to have a dad. I never thought about what it would be like to have a dad. I didn't have a reason to think that I would ever meet my dad. *At least not here on earth! Maybe in heaven, depending on if he made it there or not.* The reality was that I honestly met my dad. I had a dad. We started out good. I would call him. He would call me. One day, I realized that I was calling him more than he was calling me. I felt like I was putting more effort in getting to know him than he was putting in getting to know me. *Didn't he know that he who finds a daughter finds a good thing and has favor from the Lord! I'm just saying.*

He invited me to his church one Sunday and he got me to stand up as a visitor. He told the congregation that I was a graduate from a prominent university and that I worked for a television station. He sounded like a proud dad. As I stood there, I was thinking that he didn't even know me. He was just doing this for show. He was bragging about me as if he knew me. I was upset. I wanted to tell the whole church that I just met this man. I wanted to tell them that their beloved deacon was a fraud. In actuality, he wasn't a fraud. *My dad was HOT before it was a thing!* If you asked him anything about his kids, his past, etc., he would honestly, openly and transparently tell you the truth with no shame.

So what was my real issue sitting there in that church? For years, I held it all inside. I hadn't dealt with any of the issues surrounding my dad. I was being Miss Optimistic and not facing anything. My family was used to not talking about issues. We were used to not having deep conversations about what we were feeling or why we felt the way we did. We swept things under the rug and we didn't bring them up. And don't you dare try to look under that rug. It wouldn't matter because my family put the heaviest things that they could find and placed it over that rug.

I obviously didn't have abandonment issues when I thought this man, Daddy Dearest, was dead but now that he was alive, I had some type of serious issues going on. I still had lingering questions and my dad was ready to talk about it all, but I think that I wasn't. I knew it would be one sided. My dad was human and I knew that I would only get the side of the story that made him look the best. What would getting all these answers do anyway? How would it change the dynamic of my relationship with my mom? She was the only parent that I knew. Even though I lived a difficult life, a poor life, a life where my mom struggled to make ends meet, I wouldn't have traded it for anything. I appreciated my mom. I didn't always understand her, but I appreciated how strong she was. I didn't know what she had to deal with in life. I didn't know why she did the things she did. I didn't know why she didn't show love like other mothers. I didn't have to understand it. I knew that I loved my mom, even when it didn't feel like she loved me back.

The word of God didn't tell me that I had to understand my mother. It didn't tell me that if she did everything right that I'm supposed to honor and love her. It told me that I'm to honor and love her. *Period!* Now that I had a father, I had to honor and love him as well. Going through this whole situation, I knew I needed God. I needed His love. I needed Him to show me the way. There were times when I was talking to my dad and my emotions would stir up. We had so much in common that we would constantly butt heads. It wasn't him. It was me. *No, I'm not taking the blame for any of this. I felt like I had a right to have my moments.* After praying one day, God showed me that I was hurt. There was no sweeping it under the rug and forgetting about the fact that I didn't have a dad for my entire life. I was hurt. I was hurt by him. I was hurt by my mom. I was just hurting. I thought I was good. I was a strong, resilient young woman who had been so blessed. I was a survivor that could take on the world but some moments I would feel weak and small. I had moments of anger thinking about how we didn't have food to eat sometimes while my dad was probably somewhere enjoying a steak dinner. Thoughts like those made it difficult for me to talk to him. I would be good on the phone with him one moment and then I would get emotionally triggered. The conversation would make a left turn for the worse.

After my mom wouldn't talk to me about my dad, I started asking him questions. He ended up telling me that he tried to take my mom to court so that he could see me. He even went to put himself on child support. She never showed up to court. I knew that he wasn't lying about that part because it sounded just like her. I love her but I know her. There was no way she was showing up at a courthouse. While hearing these stories, I would get mad at my mom all over again. I would get mad at my dad as well because this just brought to light that he didn't try hard enough to see me. He told me a story about when he came to see me when I was no older than seven years old. He told me that he came to my house and asked my mom if he could take me to McDonald's. She told him no. *I don't blame her. He was basically a stranger to me. Alright, he was a complete stranger to me.* I still kept thinking that he could have tried harder.

    I needed some counseling, but more importantly I needed God to come and fix my broken heart. He did just that. I had to be honest with God and with my counselor. I had to be honest, open and transparent. I told God that I needed Him. If I was going to love my mother and father, I needed Him. 1 Peter 4:8 says "And above all things have fervent charity among yourselves: for charity shall cover the multitude of sins." Charity covers the multitude of sin. I needed a love like that. I needed to show my parents love like that. The more time that I spent with God, I was able to realize that we all sin and fall short of the glory of God. I was no better than them. How dare I judge my mother and my father? Their stuff was just that, their stuff. I didn't have anything to do with it. They had their reasons for what they did and did not do. I had to do what I thought was best for me. And what was best for me was to move past that hurt and pain and love them. When my mindset changed, I began to have better conversations with my dad. Our relationship began to grow. My love for him began to grow when I took the attention off of him and the past and focused on what God expected out of me. God made the difference.

    We ended up having a lot in common. He loves horses. I love horses. In fact, he owns several horses. *I had to fight the urge to think about how that could've been money to help me in college. Let's remember that I'm still incredibly petty.* True enough, thoughts would come up but I had to fight them. I needed God to continuously help me to take the negative thoughts captive. God did just that. I began to focus on good thoughts. I began to think about how my dad was a blessing.

    One weekend, my dad and I took a road trip to pick up a horse from his friend's ranch in Mississippi. We stayed the night and I realized that was my first time sleeping under the same roof with my dad. There I was, thirty-five years old and finally in the same house with my dad. You would have thought I was five years old the way that I was acting like daddy's little girl. I was enjoying every moment. God had brought me such a long way. We had an amazing weekend. We went to a concert. It wasn't a Gospel or Christian concert. *Don't judge me and my daddy.* It was a popular R&B singer's concert and he called us out for being at his concert together. A daughter and father sitting in the front row of that slow jam concert was a recipe for some jokes. *There will be haters everywhere.* You gotta love those memories though.

God showed me that if I had not healed from the past and learned to love unconditionally that I wouldn't have had one of the greatest moments of my life with my dad. If I had not believed that God was working through me to show my mom and dad unconditional love, I wouldn't have been able to heal and forgive. I would have missed out on moments that I can't get back. Time is so precious. I know several people including my mom and her siblings, who have lost their parents. What some people wouldn't do to have one more day with their mother and/or father. Loving people beyond their flaws, loving people beyond their faults, loving people beyond their mistakes is what God desires of us. He gives us unconditional love daily. I want to have BIG love for others. Don't you?

> Honour thy father and thy mother: that thy days may be long upon the land which the Lord thy God giveth thee. ~Exodus 20:12 KJV

> And now abideth faith, hope, charity, these three; but the greatest of these is charity. ~1 Corinthians 13:13 KJV

> He healeth the broken in heart, and bindeth up their wounds. ~Psalm 147:3 KJV

Do Me A Favor

Take a moment and think about how you love others. Are you quick to love others, even after they have wronged you? Are you quick to forgive? Open your heart to love. Open your heart to forgive. Open your heart to give God your hurt and pain. Learn to move past hurt and learn to love. Make a list of people that you want to be more intentional in showing love to. Take that list and start thinking of ways to show that you love those people and then do it. We have a Heavenly Father that loves us so much that he specializes in making sure that we are taken care of. He wants the best for you. He sent His only begotten Son so that you could live free of sin, free of worry, free of condemnation, free of sorrow, free of sickness, etc. He did this for you. He did this because He loves you so much. Share that love with others.

Pray With Me

Merciful, loving God, our Father, we come to your throne of grace and mercy to say, thank you. Thank you for loving us with an everlasting love. Thank you for showing us what it means to love. Father God, you gave your only begotten Son for us that we would have an everlasting life. What greater love is there? Thank you for the perfect sacrifice, your Son, Jesus Christ. God, we need you to help us love others. If we've been hurt and it seems as if we can't move past the pain, show us your love even more. Help us to show that love to others. If we feel like we can't forgive, help us to show your mercy. Just as you have forgiven us, help us to forgive others. Help us to genuinely love ourselves and others. When we don't feel like we deserve your love, help assure us that it's not about what we deserve. Help us to know and believe that you are a good, good father who cares so much for each of us, your children. Help us to believe that it's your love that will help us to show others grace. It's your love that will move mountains in our lives. You are able to heal us where we're broken. Only you are able to mend our hearts. We love you Lord because you first loved us. Thank you for loving us. In the name of Jesus, we pray. Amen.

Chapter 7

BIG MERCY

LAMENTATIONS 3:22-23 KJV SAYS "IT IS OF THE Lord's mercies that we are not consumed, because his compassions fail not. They are new every morning: great is thy faithfulness." I am extremely thankful for God's mercy, which is new every morning. You see, there are times in my life when I totally didn't consult God to help me figure out what His will was. I'm not talking about asking Him what type of juice I should buy or what to wear. *I actually sometimes do that now though. Let me remind you that this is a judgment free zone.* I am talking about life decisions that I know I should have prayed and consulted God about. Life decisions like getting engaged. Life decisions like getting married. You know, consulting God about who the person is that I should walk down the aisle to. Oh and when I should do it. The times that I stepped out of God's will for my life and did my own thing, I definitely needed His mercy. Each time it definitely turned out bad for me. There were times when I deserved punishment, but instead God stepped in with his undeserving, unmerited mercy, grace and favor.

I was twenty-five years old and my twenty year old boyfriend asked me to marry him. *Lord, have mercy. Lord, take pity on me. Lord, show me your compassion. You're going to hear that a lot in this chapter so just get ready for it.* Now before you say red flag #1, due to the age difference, let me defend myself. In my defense, he was turning twenty-two years old the following month after the wedding. *If that helps at all!* Why would I say yes? Let me give you the whole story. Let's go back to how this all began.

Why do most of the interesting, unique or bad things in my life begin either on a rainy day or with a lie? This "Lord, have mercy" situation actually all began as a lie. Not a bad lie, but a good lie. *Oh that sounds so horrible.* When I say a good lie, I mean the kind of lie that you tell for good. *Oh that sounds worse. It's probably best just to let that go.* I'll explain it this way. I have always looked out for other people. I am a natural helper who tries to put myself in other people's shoes. It will all make sense in a moment.

Follow me down this long rabbit trail. I had an ex-boyfriend from high school that I still kept in touch with because I was really close with his family. When I say really close with his family I mean that I called his mom "Mom" and his dad "Dad". I started babysitting his sister when I was in junior high. As the years went by, I grew closer and closer to the family. Oddly enough, the ex-boyfriend became like a brother to me. I would actually call him my brother. He didn't quite like when I called him that but I didn't care. He was family to me. *That ship had sank and drowned deeper than the Titanic so we were never, ever getting back together.* He was in the military. He moved out of town so I didn't see him or even talk to him much. If he came to town while I was at his parents' house, it would be cool. We joked on each other like siblings and kept it moving.

It was cool until this one time when he brought his new girlfriend to town. It was Thanksgiving and we were all gathering at good ole Mom and Dad's. There were name plates at each place setting on the table and someone put me at the same table as my ex and his new girlfriend. *Talk about awkward. I was good, but I don't think she was.* I tried to be as friendly as possible. She was nice in my face, but who knows except for her boyfriend how she really felt about me. It was just not the best situation. I was determined to never be in that situation again. Well, I failed. My ex-boyfriend's sister, who I babysat for years, was graduating from high school and there was no way that I was missing her graduation. I went to the house and long and behold there was my ex-boyfriend and his fiancé. *I'm sure the engagement had nothing to do with me, but I like to sometimes think the world revolves around me. I probably made them get closer after that Thanksgiving dinner.*

Once again being in the same awkward situation that I was in less than six months ago, I decided to make things better with a lie. The graduate, also known as my little sister, had a boyfriend. Her boyfriend had a friend. His friend was nicely dressed and seemed nice. *There was a lot of niceness going on.* I asked him to pretend to be my boyfriend for the night. I explained the situation and he was down for the cause, *in actuality down for the lie.* He played the part very well. You would have thought we had known each other for years instead of just a little over an hour. We sat by each other at the graduation and no one was the wiser. Well, that lie started this whole mess. By the end of the night, we exchanged numbers and long story short, we started dating.

I won't bore you with the fun-filled whirlwind of a romance we had. *That would be a book all by itself and there wouldn't be a lot of scripture in it.* After dating for almost a year, we were engaged and then a year after that we got married. Were there signs that I shouldn't have gotten married? Yes, hands down. *Before, after and on our wedding day is a great example of "I should've called that wedding off".* There were many signs, but most of them I obviously ignored.

First of all, it rained. What exactly is up with me and rain! I almost died in my car accident when it was raining. Now, here I was on my wedding day and you already know. Yes, it was raining. Strike One! I was kind of a Bridezilla so let me just tell you that any weather other than a completely clear and sunny day was only going to intensify my bad attitude. There was absolutely nothing Christ-like about me during my engagement. *I'm exaggerating only a little bit.* Anything that could go wrong was going wrong on what was supposed to be the happiest day of my life. Being happy was nowhere near this situation. I definitely would not describe my wedding as a happy occasion for me. I would not say I was filled with God's joy on that day. I should've been but I honestly wasn't.

My bridal party and I met at my favorite aunt and uncle's house. My aunt was absolutely amazing. She has always been like another mother to me. She could read me extremely well. She knew I was bothered that day. My aunt has one of those soothing voices. Her voice is gentle and kind. She puts me at peace just by talking to me. Well, that day even my aunt couldn't get through to me. I'll never forget that my necklace broke. My new necklace that had been in the box since I bought it actually broke when I was putting it on. *How was that even possible?* Strike Two! Now true enough my amazing aunt fixed my necklace, but that was definitely a strike. *God bless my aunt even though it should've stayed broken so I would reconsider the decision to get married.*

We headed to the chapel and everything seemed to be back on track. I remember being so nervous. My heart was pounding that whole day. Maybe my heart knew something that my mind didn't want to hear. The procession began. My uncle, who has always been the father figure in my life, walked me down the aisle. *In case you're wondering, yes, I asked my dad but he had something to do on that* day. *My uncle was always going to walk me down the aisle even if my dad said yes. I just wanted to put that out there.*

As we were walking down the aisle, my uncle said something to me that I'll never forget. My wonderful and hilarious uncle said, "You know you don't have to do this. We can turn around." I'm used to him joking. I think I get my sense of humor partially from him. He's the uncle that makes all the embarrassing jokes. You know the ones where I bring a different guy to the house for the holidays and he tells them that he hopes to see them the following holiday. *Well, it's not really a joke because most of the time they don't make it to the next holiday.* My uncle is just hilarious. Well at that moment, I laughed off what he said and proceeded down the aisle. *Maybe it wasn't a joke. Maybe God was using him.*

Out of all the times that I've been a drama queen, now would've been the best time to just storm out in a big dramatic way. If I had of done that it would've been the highlight of my life and that would have made this chapter way more entertaining. But instead, I continued to walk down the aisle to a man that I wanted to change. I had a whole list of things that I wanted to change about him. I knew we didn't add up to ever becoming the Godly, power couple that God had shown me.

During the ceremony, I think God was trying to give me a sign to stop. *Okay, I don't think, I actually know.* You know the signs and wonders that He shows us along the way to help guide us. They were there on my wedding day. When it was time to light the unity candle, we couldn't find it. *Now, wait, let me make this clear to you. The unity candle was in plain sight of everyone except us.* The unity candle was on the side of the altar and we didn't see it so we skipped that part. I call it a sign. Obviously at the time, I didn't realize it was a sign because I said "I do" in spite of there being no unity. *Absolutely no unity!* I was officially a wife, his wife. *What had I done?*

We argued way more than any couple should. Yes, I believe that couples have disagreements and argue but what we did was on a whole other level. He was still in college. We lived in different cities. We were four, almost five years apart in age. It didn't seem like a big deal when we met. In fact, when we met, I thought he was my age. He dressed like a mature man. He was suave. He was in the military.

At the reception we didn't walk around together like a newly, happily married couple. *Well, it's probably because we weren't.* He went his way and greeted people and I went mine. We came together for the photo ops. We came together for our first dance, which was offbeat and awkward. *Well, wait, that may have been because I didn't have much rhythm.* The photographer took a candid photo while we were dancing. The photos looked the way I felt. I'd like to think I was a beautiful bride but I wasn't smiling a lot. I was an unhappy beautiful bride who was faking my smile when I did glance one. I actually looked like I was aching on the inside. And to be honest, I was. They say a photo speaks a thousand words or something like that. That photo said a lot and most of the words were bad.

The aching turned to anger when my new husband and his fraternity brothers turned our reception into a step show. They circled around me and sang their fraternity song. I felt so special and cared for. That was planned and I knew that was going to happen. When the music came on and they began to step, I didn't know where that came from. At first, it was cute. Most of the groomsmen were his line brothers so they were all dressed up and stepping. After ten minutes, it was not so cute anymore. After twenty minutes, I was standing there alone, getting more furious. Women were cheering and taking pictures, even recording them stepping and dancing. *No, I'm not saying there is anything wrong with stepping at a wedding. I don't need anybody saying that I said you shouldn't step at a reception. You know how people spill the tea.* The issue for me was when the whole reception focused on the fraternity instead of celebrating the supposedly happy couple. *I am just speaking my truth and how I felt at the time. You have a right to your opinion.*

Long story short, it ended. Yes, the reception ended. Also, the mess of a marriage ended less than two years after that. No surprise. *People were probably betting on how long it would last anyway. All the church ladies were gambling. Whoever bet a year and eight months, literally won.* The marriage did not have Christ as the foundation. It was bound to fail. All the drama. All the tears. All the lies. All the secrets. All the heartache. All for a lesson and actually it was worth it. I have no regrets. I know I would not be who I am without that season. I learned about God's mercy. I learned that I was loved unconditionally by my heavenly father. Even though I made a decision that may not have pleased God, he covered me. If you walk in the wilderness long enough, you'll learn something while you're there. You'll come out different.

I remember when I was contemplating getting a divorce. I finally knew my worth and I wasn't going to stand for being played over any longer. I sat in my office and talked to God. I told him that I knew He hated divorce and if He wanted me to stay in that mess of a marriage I would, but if it was His will to let me out of it, to show me it was alright to make that decision. *I was pleading like I was asking him to get me out of jail. That's what the marriage felt like at that point.* I asked him to let me be alright financially. After I finished talking to God, I literally felt moved to pick up the phone and call my insurance company. The insurance representative told me once a member; always a member and that she would help me see what options I had if I was indeed getting a divorce. I started getting quotes. My homeowners insurance went down. I was going to be able to refinance my house and my mortgage was going down. I was going to be fine. The reality was that I bought the house. My husband was a college student. I paid the bills before he started working. How had I lost sight of that? *I may have been blind, but now I could see.* I was ready to move on.

After counseling, self-evaluation and soul searching, I came to the conclusion that I never wanted to marry my ex-husband. I loved his parents. His mom and dad treated me like I was their daughter. I loved his family. *It's true that you don't marry the family.* I finally came to the conclusion that I just didn't want to end up like my mom. She was never married. She had three kids out of wedlock to three different men. *No judgment. I just didn't want that life. Remember, I've fought to be the complete opposite of her.* I don't ever recall us talking about getting married before he popped the big question. I remember going to his parent's house and right there in their den, he asked me to marry him. At least he invited my favorite cousin who was there for support. *She may have been there to watch me say no.* Instead, I said yes after I whispered in his ear, "Are you serious?" Why did I say "yes"? What would make me say "yes" when I knew that something wasn't right? I think that at the time I ignored a lot. I swept every red flag that I saw under the rug. I actually swept flags of all colors that I saw under the rug. *What is up with these rugs? I inherited that sweeping things under the rug.*

I thought I was in love. I thought he would change. I thought I would change. I thought we would change. I had to learn that God does the transforming. God had to be the priority. Seek the kingdom first and then all these things will be added to you. I believe that God created marriage to glorify him. Our mess of a marriage was not doing that in any form or fashion. It was not a marriage that glorified the Lord. The very short lived, never should've happened marriage lasted less than two years. We lived together less time than that thanks to a deployment where I got back to my foundation, God. For me, I don't blame my ex-husband. I assume he did the best that he could do. People only do what you allow them to do. I should've known better. *Lord, have mercy.*

After my divorce, I was talking to God and I was literally pleading with Him. I was asking him to forgive me. Telling Him that I knew better, but I still married someone that I knew He had not chosen for me. In tears, having an ugly, ugly cry moment, I thanked God for releasing me from that marriage. I felt His arms around me. I felt Him telling me, "Daughter, you are loved. I got you. I will never forsake you. I will never leave you even when you try to go your own way." I told God that I would patiently wait on Him to bring the man that He has for me. What happened next was remarkable? I heard God tell me that I never told Him what I desired in a mate. *To be clear and keep it HOT, I heard him in my spirit, not audibly. I don't want to mislead anybody.*

Well, I picked up a pen and paper and started making a list. I kept writing and writing and writing. When I was done the list was 124 things that I desired in a mate. *The Lord had His work cut out for Him.* The next thing I heard after completing this list was "Now let those things be in you first". *Wait. Hold up. This list would have been a lot shorter if I knew that God wanted me to be what I wrote down first.* You see on that list there were things like Christ-like, humble, forgiving, patient, etc. I was twenty-eight years old and I was really struggling with about two-thirds of that list. Honestly, it was probably more than that. *I was good with the things like Alabama fan, great sense of humor, ambitious and no children but the rest. Oh my!* The things I desired in a mate had to first be in me. I heard God loud and clear *in my spirit*. It was time for me to embrace my single life and work on me.

I will tell you that there were many moments of wilding out. For a HOT moment, I will tell you that even though I was reading the word, going to church and truly trying, really striving to be

Christ-like, I was nowhere near it. I was a total disappointment before the ink was dry on my divorce papers. I had been so thankful to God. I felt blessed to be out of my mess of a marriage and there I was being a hot mess. *That's a whole other book by itself.* It doesn't take long for God to grab me and bring me to complete surrender. He did just that. By almost the end of the following year, I was hanging around a new group of people. I was doing a discipleship. I had great spiritual leaders. I believed that I was truly making God smile. Mercy and grace was covering me.

Let's fast forward to ten years after my divorce. I was indeed living my best single life, very single life. Who cares about the title divorcee? Not me. I was focused on my career. I was traveling. I was helping my brother with my niece who I took in. I could care less that people were telling me that since I was single with no kids and approaching forty years old that I needed to find a husband. *First of all, my husband is going to find me. Secondly, I'm not looking for my husband. Thirdly, God is going to send my husband when it's time.* If I was meant to be like Paul, I was kind of, sort of ready. It definitely was not the route I would have chosen but I was not going to settle for a guy that I knew God hadn't sent. I talked to guys. I even dated some guys, but nothing clicked. One year, I dated Jesus. I literally dated Jesus. I wore a ring on my ring finger. I told people I was dating JC/Jesus Christ. We went on dinner dates and movie dates. We had the best conversations. We took trips together. *If you're judging me, it's cool. My friends and coworkers did as well. Those were fun times, people, fun times.*

After being married to someone that I knew God didn't choose for me, I knew that I wanted to date for the purpose of marriage. I felt like guys knew what they wanted when they met a female. I was told in college by one of my guy friends that a guy knows soon after he meets you whether he wants to just be cool with you, if he wants you to be his girlfriend, if he could see himself marrying you or if he just wants to sleep with you. There is not any data to support this theory, but it is ingrained in my thoughts when I meet a guy.

By some miracle, I met a guy. *Me and my long list of standards actually met a guy.* I wasn't looking for him as suggested by hundreds of people. I simply went to a family day event that my cousin was hosting for his work staff. At that event, I met this great guy. *Well, they all seem to start out that way. Just kidding! Kinda!* I want to reiterate that I was definitely not looking for a guy. I was happy with where I was in life and then he came. Since my divorce, I had my fair share of failed relationships. I had some flings, some distractions, and some stupid decisions. I had some waste of time, some hesitation, some frustration, and some fornication situations. *Just keeping it HOT.*

At that point in my life, I was approaching forty years old and I knew what God expected out of me. I also knew what he didn't expect out of me. It was simple. Strive daily to be more Christ-like. Forgive myself. Forgive others. Embrace mercy and repent. Represent him. Show love to others. If I was not going to allow all of that to be part of my relationship with a guy there was no need to be in one. I did not need a relationship. I desired a relationship. There is a huge difference. Saying that I did not need a relationship did not mean that I was so independent and since I had my own that I didn't need a relationship. *I had to hear numerous people tell me how intimidating I could seem, especially making that statement. Whatever! Not needing a relationship means that I can stand on my own and if God doesn't bring the man that he has for me then I'm good. Desiring a relationship means that I didn't need one, but I wanted one.*

The relationship with this guy was different. The time came when I spiritually matured and I wanted a relationship pleasing to God. I wanted to be married before having sex so I made that clear to this guy. *I was officially a reformed fornicator. If there is such a thing!* Surprisingly, he was all for it. He said that I was worth waiting for. Alright now! That was music to my ears. *He was one of the few guys that didn't run when I confessed my celibacy. True that we all sin and fall short but I didn't want that one on my list anymore. I'm just saying.*

We ended up getting into a relationship pretty quickly. How quickly? *I'm glad you asked.* Like I met him on a Saturday and in about three days, he said I was the one. I just went with the flow. I was big on a guy being the leader. As long as he was being prayerful about our direction, I would be good. We prayed together. He cooked for me and invited me over to his house. We enjoyed each other's company. We started going to church together. It was great. We signed up for relationship counseling with my pastor. A little before our first session, he proposed. We had been dating for a little less than four months with no sex. I thought it was an answered prayer when he asked me. I prayed that God would send me a guy who knew what he wanted and it wouldn't take long for him to commit to me. *I really need to be more careful and specific with my prayers.*

We started planning the wedding and things began to change. We would go to our relationship counseling sessions and I would cry. I just didn't have any peace. He would get in these moods. He would be closed off a lot. He wasn't honest about his financial situation. He seemed to not be honest with who he was. His representative didn't last long. About three or four months after our engagement, God closed the door on that relationship. "*God closed the door*" *as church folks say. You know instead of saying you had another failed relationship, you got dumped or you lost your job or got fired.* Keeping it HOT, I know that God saved me from making yet another mistake of marrying a man just because he proposed.

The sad thing is that each time I stepped out on my own; I ended up asking for forgiveness and saying "Lord, please have mercy on me". I do not know who can relate to that but if you're being **H**onest, **O**pen and **T**ransparent, you probably can admit that you've definitely said it. I did not know that my marriage or my engagement would end up as "Lord, please have mercy on me" relationships. I was the young lady that knew God. I prayed. I attended church. And let's not forget that I was the miracle child who had been saved less than a decade prior to making the brave decision to get married. A decade after that, I made the brave decision to get married again. *Lord, have mercy on me.*

After truly believing that God was working on my behalf in each situation, I knew that he wanted the best for me. I knew that I had freewill to make decisions and that I needed to be in close relationship with Him to know what to do and when to do it. I couldn't be fearful. As a result, I didn't fear being like my mom anymore. God did not give me a spirit of fear, but of a sound mind. My sound mind helped me to make better decisions when entering into relationships. Single or married, I know that I am loved. I am chosen. I am accepted. I am special. *Sometimes you just have to encourage yourself: "You is kind. You is smart. You is important."* God's mercy and love continues to follow me daily. When I think about relationships and life in general, I say thank you Lord for having BIG mercy on me.

> But thou, O Lord, art a God full of compassion, and gracious, long suffering, and plenteous in mercy and truth. ~Psalm 86:15 KJV

> The Lord is gracious, and full of compassion; slow to anger, and of great mercy. [9] The Lord is good to all:

and his tender mercies are over all his works. ~Psalm 145:8-9 KJV

It is of the Lord's mercies that we are not consumed, because his compassions fail not. ²³ They are new every morning: great is thy faithfulness. ~Lamentations 3:22-23 KJV

DO ME A FAVOR

Have you ever said, "Lord, please have mercy on me."? Focus on that time or multiple times. *You know I'm not judging. I definitely don't have any room to judge even if I wanted to.* I want you to focus on God's mercy. Do you believe that God's mercy is new every morning? Or is it just something you say because you read it? Do you truly, truly believe that God's mercy is new every single day and that His mercy is for you? He is freely giving it to you. He knows you're going to need it. He knows you're going to need it each and every day. Are you willing to receive God's mercy every day? It makes a big difference in our lives when we can receive God's mercy and grace knowing that He didn't send His son to condemn us. Embrace God's mercy and let go.

PRAY WITH ME

Father God, Lord of mercy, King of kings, we come to you to say thank you for your grace and your mercy that you give to us freely every morning. We are grateful for the never-ending, new mercy that we receive. We do not know where we would be without it. For the times that we have gone left when you told us to go right, we ask for forgiveness. We thank you for keeping us even in those moments of disobedience. We trust your word which tells us that nothing can separate us from your love. The enemy wants us to believe that you love us less when we step out of your will, but we're so grateful that we know that you never love us any less. Father, when we think about the mistakes that we've made, the mistakes that we continue to make, help us to not dwell on them. Because of your mercy we know that nothing can separate us from your love. Nothing can separate us from you. You sent your only begotten son for us. Thank you that because of you, we do not live in condemnation. Thank you that even when we fail by our definition, you pick us up and let us know that we have your mercy. We are not held captive by our sin because you sent your son to set us free. You know us and love us flaws and all. We praise and thank You for how you see us for who we are, sometimes Father, mess and all, and you choose to embrace us completely. You knew us before we were ever formed in our mother's womb. Thank you God for being loving and compassionate towards us, your children. Your mercy reveals exactly how just and fair you are, but also how loving and compassionate you are. Because of the mercy that you give us, we're able to show mercy to others. We declare and decree that we will be merciful unto others because we continue to receive your mercy daily. Father, help us each day to show mercy to others. In the name of Jesus! It's not easy, but with you all things are possible. We love you, Father God, because you first loved us. Thank you for your abundant mercy. Thank you for your unconditional love. In the name of Jesus, we pray. Amen.

Chapter 8
BIG HEALING

I'M PROUD TO SAY THAT THE ONLY BROKEN bones I've ever had were in my neck. Growing up, some of the kids I went to school with would break their arm or leg and then come to school with a cast on. I thought their casts were so cool. I would sign people's cast with a Sharpie. *The good ole days!* We didn't have health insurance so I basically couldn't afford to get hurt. I definitely couldn't afford to break any bones. Now that I think about it, I couldn't really afford to catch a cold. I can recall catching a cold and my mom would rub Vicks vapor rub on my chest after a scorching hot bath. *I'm really surprised I didn't get third degree burns from that water.* She would put a little under my nose and she would make me swallow a little. Years later, I read the warning label and it said for external use only. *Thanks a lot Ma! I know for sure that God's grace is sufficient.*

Growing up with no health insurance and not being able to go to the doctor or dentist made me eager to schedule appointments as soon as I became an adult and landed a job with health benefits. Good health insurance changed my life. I made sure that I made my annual appointments and kept them. With my family having a history of heart disease and strokes, I was diligent with trying to stay healthy. My mom always said that going to the doctor is what made you sick and that she would rather not know if anything is wrong with her. She said it would only make you worry and that would make you even sicker. *Whatever! I was definitely not a proponent of that at all.*

Well, worrying was something that I never had to worry about. *No pun intended.* I was constantly working out and doing what my doctors told me to do. I was never anxious when it came to my health because I always had a good report. I took care of my temple. I was constantly fasting even before my church asked us to do a corporate fast. *No shade intended.* Health and wellness was at the top of the list of my priorities. Worrying when it came to my body was non-existent. Well things changed drastically after one of my gynecologist appointments.

All I could hear was my friend telling me to not worry until you have a reason to worry. I was sitting in my gynecologist's office with my legs crossed waiting for him to come in and tell me what he saw on my ultrasound. I had been having some abdominal pain for a while, but the pain wasn't unbearable so I didn't have the time to deal with it. My ex-husband used to say that pain is weakness leaving the body. I hated when he said it but for some reason it stuck with me. I started saying it and living by it. *It's just sad the things that stayed with me from that "Lord, have mercy" season in my life.* Let me tell you that if pain is weakness leaving the body, I was really weak for months and the pain was supposed to be gone. As much as I was dealing with pain in my back, side, stomach and abdomen, I did not want to slow down. I actually would not have been sitting in the doctor's office at that moment if they had not found something strange when I had my annual exam. That uncomfortable but necessary Pap smear led me to having an ultrasound. I used to only associate ultrasounds with pregnancy but that all changed. *I definitely wasn't pregnant unless it was another miracle of God, another Messiah that God placed in the womb. Even if you could get pregnant from kissing, I still wouldn't have been pregnant. I'm just saying.*

The news wasn't good. They found uterine fibroids. The sizes of the fibroids ranged. The largest was a little larger than a tennis ball. *What the what! To be honest, I didn't know if this was good or bad. I didn't even know what fibroids were.* I knew they didn't belong in my body. I knew that they were the culprit of all the pain I felt. Several questions started forming as my physician started explaining about these foreign objects in my uterus. He explained that uterine fibroids were noncancerous growths. No cancer means good news. He said they came from a genetic disposition. *Other people inherit money and good things, but I would get some fibroids.* They were treatable. Great news! They could grow in number and size if not treated. That's bad news. *I imagined a whole takeover in my uterus.* I was thirty-six years old and I had never tried to have a baby. *Let's remember that "Lord, have mercy" marriage that I know I wasn't supposed to be fruitful and multiply anything in.* If God ever, I mean ever brought the man that he had for me into my life, were the fibroids going to stop me from having a baby? They were in there taking up a lot of space.

My physician explained that my uterus was larger because of the fibroids. I knew this wasn't good. We were looking at having surgery. I trusted my physician. More than anything, I trusted God. Sitting in that room, I was confident. I was strong. I had no fear. By the time I left out the door of the office and made it to my car, I had a total meltdown. I cried. I called my favorite cousin who is a minister to have a real moment, an honest moment. She said everything that I needed to hear at that moment. Most importantly, she prayed with me. Of course, I cried some more, but I knew that God was in control. I had so many questions. I just didn't understand what was going on. As many questions that I had, I believed that He had answers.

I had to go back to my office after that appointment and I told my boss what was going on. I was so thankful that I worked for a faith-based workplace. My boss prayed with me. I felt more relief for a moment. I actually forgot about the pain that I had been feeling. In fact, the pain didn't even feel as bad as it usually did. Maybe God was healing me without surgery. *I believed Him for the impossible yet again. I survived being underwater for 10 minutes with a broken neck. God could definitely handle these fibroid things.*

I had to schedule my surgery, also known as a myomectomy to be exact. I was going to have to be off of work for six weeks. *Ain't nobody got time for that!* I had been on my job for almost 11 years without missing any real time off. I didn't go on my first full weeks' vacation until the year before all of this mess. I was the community events manager for a hospital system. I managed an average of ninety to a hundred events a year. I worked over half the weekends in the year. I worked seven, eight, nine days straight. Now, thanks to some surgery, I was going to have to take time off of work. What could God possibly be showing me? What was there to learn or gain from this situation? Whether I liked it or not, my surgery was scheduled and I had about four months to come up with a plan to be off of work. I thought that would be my only problem, but it wasn't.

They say when it rains it pours. *We all know by now how I feel about rain anyway.* I don't even like to use that expression. They say if it ain't one thing, it's another. I don't like to use that expression either. I'm too optimistic for those sayings or so I thought. As I sat in my neurosurgeon's office with neck pain, I was thinking about those sayings. *And on all days, it just had to be Valentine's Day.* I had found out what was causing the pain in my back and abdomen and I was getting that resolved in a couple of months. But then I just had to have some neck pain that started getting worse. *Yes, it had been hurting for a while, but I didn't have time to deal with that. I'm a busy woman.* It seemed like it was so much easier to just live with the pain. I couldn't live with it any longer though. And with the same neurosurgeon that did the fusion on my neck and helped save my life having an office right around the corner of the hallway from my office, I knew I couldn't get away with hiding this pain for much longer. I talked to him and that's how I ended up in his physician practice office. He saw my scans from my primary physician. There was absolutely no surprise that he wanted to see me in his office as soon as possible. He wanted to check me out for himself after seeing my scan.

My neurosurgeon who was one of my favorite physicians in our hospital system was always honest with me. He knew my history. He knew me. He looked at the scan and he told me that there was no way that I wasn't in pain at that moment. He said that because of my previous fusion on C4 and C5 that he had done a little over twenty years ago that I was experiencing a bulge in C6. This was not good news. He proceeded to tell me that if he had to go back into my neck to correct it with surgery, it would be quite a process. My neurosurgeon explained to me that if he had to perform surgery that he would need to go through the front of my neck. Just the thought of that made me want to pass out. I wanted to cry, but I couldn't.

He told me that he wanted to try a couple of things first. All I needed was a little hope. All I needed was a little faith. He gave me an inch and I was going to take a mile with whatever he told me to do to avoid surgery. Out of all the things he could say, he said thirteen weeks of physical therapy. *Let's recall from Chapter 2, BIG Timing, that I hated physical therapy.* But oh baby, I was older and wiser this time around. I believed that God was telling me that I failed the test the first time, but now I had another opportunity to get it right. I was ready. I was stronger. I was determined. I was not a quitter. *It only took twenty years. Don't judge me.*

One of the perks of working for a hospital system was that I knew the physical therapists. I worked with a lot of them on projects. I was going to put in the work and God was going to do the rest. I believed that as long as I did my part, He would indeed do the rest. I believed that He would heal my neck. I believed that I wouldn't have to have cortisone injections or surgery. Faith without works is dead. I could believe all I wanted to, but without action, I was just talking. I anticipated the pain. I anticipated horrible sessions. I completely built this whole agonizing therapy situation in my head and it wasn't that bad. *This is added to the number of times I wrote a whole narrative in my head about something and it wasn't even what I imagined. Countless times! Don't judge me.*

My physical therapist was amazing and extremely kind. She took her time with me. She catered to what I needed and what I could tolerate. After thirteen weeks of therapy, I was healed. *Won't He do it!* Only God could give me the strength to get through therapy. Only God could heal my neck yet again. I had seen God work yet another miracle with me avoiding surgery. *You should've seen that scan of my neck. It was pretty bad even if I say so myself.*

It was time to face the music about my fibroids. The months were passing quickly and the pain was not getting any better. In my mind though, the closer that I got to my surgery date, I believed God for yet another healing. I remember praying and asking God to take the fibroids away. I literally thought that they would just disappear and I wouldn't have to have surgery. *This is honestly how my faith-filled mind worked.*

Something happened out of the normal the day before my surgery. My gynecologist wanted me to come to his office to have another ultrasound. He said that he just wanted to take another look before surgery the next day. His office was basically right across the street from my office so I went. It wasn't an inconvenience at all because I went in thinking that the ultrasound was not going to show any fibroids. I prayed and I spoke it out loud. I told my boss and coworkers that the fibroids were going to be gone. I knew God could do it. I believed in Him once again for the impossible. Well, they did the ultrasound and they found two more fibroids. *God has a sense of humor. I can't even make this stuff up.* I went back to my office shame-faced and told them that there was a change. I now had nine fibroids that were being removed instead of seven. It was inevitable that I was going to have surgery the next day. I hadn't had surgery since I had a broken neck and now I was going to have these fibroids removed from my uterus.

On surgery day, I didn't have any worries. I knew that God would take care of me. I knew that if He brought me to it, He was indeed going to bring me through it. I had too much work to do for His kingdom. I was walking by faith. I was really good. My mom was with me. I knew I was going to be fine. They took me to the back and prepped me. My mom was able to come to the back when they were done prepping me before they took me to surgery. My gynecologist came to my side, took my hand and prayed with me and my mom. That did it for me. I knew that I was going to be just fine.

I made it through surgery. My recovery was quick. I ended up being able to go back to work before my scheduled time. I'm an overachiever like that. Although everyone told me that I should've just taken the time and rested to make sure that I was fully recovered, I didn't listen. *A hard head makes a soft behind.* I rushed my recovery and ended up back at home for a little longer. I basically ended up almost doing the six weeks anyway. *I should've just sat down somewhere.* God definitely has a way of sitting you down. I learned my lesson and I praised Him for showing it to me. Within six months, I had thirteen weeks of physical therapy and a myomectomy. I knew God to be a healer. I needed God to heal me like He did twenty years ago after my car accident and He did. It served as a reminder of God's grace. It served as a reminder that He is the same God.

The year was almost over and I was feeling great. Well, wait. Not completely great. For some reason, I was feeling pain in my wrist and thumb. I couldn't think of what I had done to it. I just knew there wasn't going to be another thing wrong with me this year. The pain wasn't getting any better. It was my dominant hand, my right hand, so I knew that I had to go see a physician about the pain. It was becoming unbearable. I went to an orthopedic surgeon and I found out that I had yet another thing that I had never heard of. I was diagnosed with de Quervain's tenosynovitis. *Don't ask me how to pronounce it. I still can't say it right.*

To make matters worse, I was also diagnosed with a trigger thumb. I honestly thought that I was being pranked when my orthopedic surgeon told me what was going on. *I played a horrible April Fool's joke on my boss some years prior and he said he was going to get me back when I least expected it. Could this be my payback?*

This would have been the worst payback. I received a shot in my wrist that I will never forget. I will never forget that cortisone shot. It was excruciating pain. I yelled so loud in that office. *It hurt so bad that I could've slapped my mama. Wait, never mind. Not my mama.* I had to be in a splint and if it didn't get better, you already know what was next. Surgery was the next form of treatment to correct everything and relieve me of the pain. I prayed and prayed for it to get better. I believed God to be a healer. I believed that

God would take the pain away and I wouldn't have to have surgery. *At this point I was like a broken record.* My prayers would not cease though. I needed my hand to get better. I needed this hand to get healed because I couldn't use it. *How about one day, I made it all the way to my office and I looked down to find the lotion on my legs hadn't even been rubbed in all the way!* Embarrassing moment after embarrassing moment, made me pray even harder.

I went back to the orthopedic surgeon and (*drum roll*) it wasn't better. *No, it was not better. I couldn't believe it either.* They scheduled me for surgery. Was I disappointed? Yes. Did I still believe that God was with me? Yes. It didn't matter what the outcome was going to be. My mind was made up that no matter what, I was going to rejoice. I was going to give God glory because it could be worse than having surgery. I knew people who lost limbs due to diabetes. How dare I complain about having yet another surgery when some people would take what I was going through over what they were dealing with! My attitude about this surgery was going to be positive. I was going to praise God and add another testimony to my story. I had surgery on my right hand and I came through surgery like a champ. *In your face, devil!*

In less than a year, I went from not having any surgeries since the one major one that I had twenty years ago to having thirteen weeks of physical therapy to avoid spinal surgery, a myomectomy to remove nine uterine fibroids and hand surgery to repair my right thumb and wrist. It was a trying twelve months, but God gave me strength. It was a trying year but God healed me. In my own strength there was no way I could have made it through any of it, but with God's strength, I could do all things. I can't explain why all these trials happened within the time that they did, but I know that God kept me yet again. He healed me. He provided the right physicians for me. He provided insurance. He provided a great support system at work and home. He sent his word to heal me. I know that BIG healings happen.

After that year with all the trials, I was sure that I would not have to face any of those issues again. Well wouldn't you know that the following year that stupid gynecology checkup led me down the road of having another ultrasound! Another ultrasound and still not for a baby! *I might not even want an ultrasound when I get pregnant. They only bring bad news.* Well, this time, there was more bad news. The ultrasound showed that my body formed new fibroids. *Once again, thanks for that genetic disposition that caused me to have fibroids. My family really could've left something better for me. What about some money, property, and/or jewelry!*

Regardless of why I had them again, I had them again. My gynecologist explained that they weren't very large. He told me about a drug that could possibly shrink them and prevent me from having surgery yet again. I was all for it until he continued to tell me that it would put me in menopause. Now hold up, me in my late thirties in menopause. *I'm a handful without mood swings and hot flashes. Ask any of the people that really, really know me.*

I told my gynecologist that I would pray about it and find out more information before making a decision. I did just that. I asked God to tell me what to do. It was clear to me to seek good, professional, Godly counsel. I knew a pharmacist and she researched the drug for me. She told me that it might be worth trying at least for a month. The drug could only be taken for six months at a time because it decreases your bone density levels. It also causes you to have menopausal symptoms. *That wasn't going to be good for anybody. Hot flashes before I was forty years old had to be a joke. Everybody needed to mentally prepare for this.*

After praying and feeling peace, the decision was made to start the drug. I hadn't asked about the cost of the drug. *Well, I should* have. *As frugal as I am, that should've been my first question.* And wouldn't you know it, the drug was really expensive. It was almost two hundred dollars per dose. I knew that if God was leading me to take this drug that he was going to have to provide the finances. *He knew I didn't have it.* I was calling on and believing Jehovah Jireh, my provider.

My good and faithful father did just that. He provided. A nurse told me about a program that assisted with paying for the drug. It was a discount assistance program that I didn't even know existed. The cost went from two hundred dollars to twenty five dollars a dose. I only had to have one dose once a month. Only God could do that. *Won't He do it!* I ended up feeling fine after the first month. I was a little warm, a little toasty at times. If the drug was working, I could endure the fiery furnace for some months. *The hot flashes were no joke. I honestly feel like since I basically went through menopause one time, I shouldn't have to go through it again. I'm just saying!*

I continued getting shots in my hip once a month for six months. It was time for me to see if the fibroids indeed shrunk. The dreaded ultrasound took place and the results were good. The fibroids shrunk. I was excited. I was living a pain free life once again. I accredit it all to God. I believe that He worked on my behalf. He surrounded me with people that confirmed everything that he showed me. He healed me. He provided the pharmacist for me to ask questions and research the drug. He provided a program to offset the cost of the expensive drug. He sent his word yet again to heal me. I know that BIG healings happen.

In full disclosure, I want to let you know that as I write this book, my body has formed new fibroids. *Yes, thanks genetics and whatever else I have going on.* I have fibroids yet again. This is a fight that I may have to continue fighting until I die or remove my uterus. *Some days a hysterectomy sounds good so whichever comes first.*

This fight has taught me a lot about my body. I have learned about fibroids. Prior to having them, I never heard of uterine fibroids. Now that I know, now that I live with them, I take any opportunity to share my experience and to bring awareness to fibroids. Let's get educated. Fibroid awareness month is July. Each year, I want you to wear white to bring awareness to this health issue that affects millions of women. I bet you know someone who has fibroids. *You would be surprised.* There are many women who don't even know that they have them. *I didn't.*

> Heal me, O LORD, and I shall be healed; save me, and I shall be saved: for thou art my praise.
> ~Jeremiah 17:14 KJV

> But he was wounded for our transgressions, he was bruised for our iniquities: the chastisement of our peace was upon him; and with his stripes we are healed.
> ~Isaiah 53:5 KJV

> Not that I speak in respect of want: for I have learned, in whatsoever state I am, therewith to be content. [12] I know both how to be abased, and I know how to abound: everywhere and in all things I am instructed both to be full and to be hungry, both to abound and to suffer need. [13] I can do all things through Christ which strengtheneth me. ~Philippians 4:11-13 KJV

Do Me A Favor

Answer this question for me: Are you in need of a healing today? I don't want you to only think about healing in the physical sense. That may be the case for some of you, but remember that God can heal you emotionally, financially, mentally, physically, spiritually. If you are in need of healing, I want you to fully submit that request to God. Begin to let go and let God. You cannot do it on your own. I think about the times that I tried to do things on my own. It was exhausting. Look to God the one who knows all. You are the one who supplies all our needs. He is waiting for you to ask. He is waiting on you to fully surrender that need to him.

Pray with Me

Father God, we thank you for being Jehovah Rapha, our God who heals. Our loving father who continues to heal us emotionally, financially, physically and spiritually, thank you. Father God, we thank you for the strength that comes from you and you alone. We thank you that when we are weak, you are indeed strong. If we are in need of healing today, Father God, we trust that you will heal us like only you can. Father, we know you to be Jehovah Rapha, God who heals, so I declare and decree that all is well with our bodies, our minds, our souls. Every tissue, every cell, every bone, every organ, every muscle functions just as you created it, working properly! Everything you created, Father God, is good. Because of your goodness, your grace, your faithfulness, your divine favor, we declare and decree that no disease, no illness, no disorders can prosper in our bodies. Though they may form, they will not prosper. We declare and decree 1 Peter 2:24 that says He himself bore our sins in his body on the cross, so we might die to sins and live for righteousness; by his wounds we have been healed. By every stripe, every lash, we are healed. Thank you, Father God, for your son, Jesus Christ that you sent for us. I declare and decree that we are covered by the precious blood of Jesus. Jesus Christ who died for us. What greater love than a man who would lay down his life! Thank you for your son who set us free through his perfect sacrifice. May our bodies be a reflection of Him. May our temples represent who He is. We declare and decree Mark 5:34 that by our faith that we are healed. We will go in peace and be freed from our suffering. We believe and receive your peace, your healing, your favor, your strength. If it is not your timing for us to be healed, give us the strength to endure. Give us the strength and courage to continue running this race. Father, I declare and decree that all is well. In the name of Jesus, we pray. Amen.

BIG FORG

One of the biggest things I've ...
my life through so many situations is that forgivene...
of life. I don't care what age you are, every person at so...
life is going to have to forgive someone or be forgiven by ...
Personally I like being on the end of having to forgive someone
asking for forgiveness but I've had my fair share of both. One of
hardest things I've had to do is forgive someone who never apo...
ogized. You know the people that have never admitted that they
were wrong. Or the people that never even admit that they did
anything against you at all. My ex-husband has never apologized
for the heartache, pain and embarrassment he caused me. It never
mattered to me about him apologizing. I forgave him before the
ink was even dry on our divorce papers. I will gladly take an "L" for
that one. I forgave him and I forgave myself. I should have never
married a twenty-one year old who wasn't ready for marriage. Did
I know he wasn't ready? No. Did I know that our relationship did
not resemble a Godly relationship? Yes. *That's actually not me being
petty but being completely honest.*

It became real apparent that when 1 Peter 5:8 says "your enemy
the devil prowls around like a roaring lion looking for someone to

…e "someone" was definitely me. I don't want to speak
…e but if you're anything like me, you know a thing or
…versity and challenges. During those challenging times,
…verses like good, old John 10:10. I memorized this verse
…I quote it all the time. John 10:10 says "The enemy comes
…ill and destroy, but I have come that they may have life
…undant". Sometimes we only focus on "the enemy comes to
…ill and destroy" also known as the "a" part of the verse. *Let me*
…eak for you though. Sometimes, I have only focused and even
…ed just the "a" part but I had to change my mindset.

True enough, the enemy, the devil, Satan is lurking seeking to
…al, kill and destroy but I have a heavenly Father watching over
…ie, protecting me. God helped me to see that there is hope in the
last part, the "b" part of John 10:10. I decided to trust the "b" part of that verse. I had to face the reality that because of my relationship with Christ that the "a" part was going to happen but Jesus also says "but I have come that they may have life and have it more abundantly". The "He" is Jesus and the "they" is us. The "they" is me. I choose to believe it's God. I take Him at His word. I believe it's God working in the midst of every situation and circumstance. When He's working, no matter what it looks like, He will make it work out for my good. Romans 8:28 says "And we know that in all things God works for the good of those who love him, who have been called according to his purpose."

How can you see God working things together for good when the enemy is attacking in every way possible? How can you see God working things together for good when the enemy is using people to hurt you? It's definitely not easy but I believe that God desires for us to cling to Him. He wants us to forgive others just as He has forgiven us. I can't count the number of times a counselor has told me forgiveness isn't for the other person, it's for you. I can't count the number of times that I've had to put my pride aside and say you're right. *Man, I'm keeping it HOT in here!*

I've mentored young girls who have told me flat out that they can't forgive the people who hurt them. I've sat down with young ladies who have been sexually abused in unimaginable ways. I had to hold back tears as I listened to one young lady tell me that her mom would sell her and her sisters to get drugs. I have had to tell them all how much God loves them in spite of what they went through. I have told them how they have to forgive their offenders and themselves. I'm honest with them to tell them that it doesn't happen overnight. It's a process. It is a process that I believe has to include God. It's a process that I myself went through.

You see God has gotten me through more than just accidents and surgeries. He saved me from losing my mind when I was a teenager. On Mother's Day at the age of fourteen, I was baptized at the church that I started visiting with my cousin. Some months after I was baptized my life changed. I'm not talking about the incredible change that I experienced from becoming a Christian. I'm talking about the horrible change that took place after my mom's boyfriend molested me. *Sorry I had to just blurt that out like that.* There really is no crafty way to say that my mom's thirty something year old boyfriend stole my virginity. *I attempted to debate with God about not including this sensitive and personal life-changing event. Obviously I lost.* He made it clear to me to include it. I will tell you right now that this was one of the hardest chapters to write. *I was literally like "God, I don't have any jokes, sarcastic remarks or witty comments to go along with this. You're just really gonna have to help me".* And yet again, God reminded me that I'm not alone and that this is going to help some people forgive and heal. He said tell the story. Keep it HOT!

There were very few times when I was growing up that one of my mom's boyfriends didn't live with us. Either we lived with them or they lived with us. *Where were they when we didn't have a place to stay? In fact this was one of the ones that put us out of his house but I digress.* My mom worked all the time. At this time, she was working at a cleaning service so she cleaned a building in the evenings into the night. It was a Friday afternoon. I made it home from school and I planned to spend the weekend at my friend's house. There was one issue. My friend's mom couldn't pick me up from my house. This was a common issue for me so I was used to it. I really wanted to go to her house. My mom's boyfriend came home. It was just me and him. It didn't happen often. Actually, I don't ever recall being alone with him at the house prior to this.

I honestly never had a good feeling about him. He was some years younger than my mom and he was just a little too friendly with me. Even at my age, I knew that it wasn't right for him to want me to sit on his lap or give him a kiss on his cheek. He smoked and I hated the smell of smoke. He would do this stuff in front of my mom so I didn't think twice about it. I would do what he said because if he was happy that meant my mom was happy. We had cable television for the first time. We were able to stay up later on school nights. We had a place to live. The bills were paid. We ate every day. He had a car. Of course I would've gladly gone without if I had a choice.

On that Friday afternoon, I asked him for a ride to my friend's house so I could spend the weekend with her. He told me that he would take me but he wanted me to do something first. He took me in my room, laid me on my pink and white floral comforter on my bed and had sex with me. I remember him kissing me and he smelt like cigarette smoke. Just like that, before I even fully understood what sex was, before I could make a decision to have sex or not, my choice was taken from me. To this day I can't remember very much afterwards. I don't remember what I was wearing. I don't remember how I felt afterwards. I remember that he told me that he put something on the fireplace for me. I went up front to the living room and there was twenty dollars lying on the fireplace. There were no words to describe how I felt. Even years later, there were days when there were no words to describe how I felt.

He did take me to my friend's house. I don't even remember much about the car ride except that he told me not to tell anyone what happened. He told me that even if I told my mom she wouldn't believe me. The sad thing is that I believed him. I always prayed to God for protection. I believe that God did just that because my mom's boyfriend never touched me again. Now there are some people that have asked me why God allowed it to happen to me at all. I honestly don't know. What I do know is that He answered my prayer. What I do know is that He covered my mind when I started having nightmares about what he did to me. I started having nightmares about never being able to have kids because of what he did to me. I was angry but I was even more confused. I blamed myself for giving him the kiss on his cheek and sitting on his lap when he asked. I couldn't talk to anyone about it. The only person I had was my heavenly father and when I tell you that He kept me. He kept me.

That man sexually abused me once, but that one time was something that I would have to live with forever. God helped me to move on. He removed the thoughts of the incident almost immediately after it happened. It's as if he blocked the memory of it. I needed that. I still had to live in the house with this man. It's literally as if God removed it from my memory. Counselors have told me that blocking the memory of the trauma is a coping mechanism. *Well, it worked. I was able to cope.* I still did well in school. I remained an honor roll student. I was able to function without fear of him.

I believed that God was protecting me. I was young, but I understood the power of prayer. *Boy, did I pray.* The Baptist church that I attended taught the Bible and my pastor didn't play. I was learning and I was applying everything that I heard. I saw God helping me. I saw God covering me every day.

One day, my prayer was answered. The man had the audacity to cheat on my mom. *Wait, I'm not counting with me. Just keeping it HOT.* He actually cheated with a woman their age. *Chump! Please Lord; forgive me for calling the man a chump.* He was younger than my mom anyway. I don't know what she saw in him. But just like that he was gone from my life. Thank you Lord. I hoped I would never see him again. Years went by and he was a distant memory. When I was twenty-five, I actually ran into him. I was a little shocked to see him again. I know that God brought me a long way because I actually said hi and kept walking. It didn't bother me at all. I refused to let that man steal anything more than he'd already taken from me.

What the enemy tried to use against me failed. I didn't feel less than. I didn't feel like a victim. I was not going to let what he did to me define me. I didn't talk about it. I didn't entertain it. I went on with life. I lived a normal teenage life. *Well, pretty normal until two years later when I was in that car accident when I was sixteen.* Other than that, I was pretty basic. I dated some. I may have become sexually active earlier than planned but I can't say that was because of what happened to me. *Who knows!* I didn't want to give any room to the enemy. I was human. I messed up. I never faltered with my relationship with God. I knew He loved me. I knew that He forgave me even in my sin. *At some point, I was bound to get it right or at least get better.*

The reality was that I was forgiven time and time again by God. He sent His son, Jesus Christ to die for me. I was sitting in church learning about forgiveness. I was saying "Amen" during sermons about forgiving others. All this time, I was still harboring unforgiveness towards the man that took so much from me. It wasn't doing me any good to be mad at him. It was not helping me to be upset. I couldn't take back what he did to me. I couldn't change anything in the past, but I could own my future. I could let go and move on. I forgave and I moved on.

At the age of nineteen, I finally told someone about my mom's boyfriend molesting me when I was fourteen years old. I was dating this guy in college and I told him what my mom's boyfriend did. I don't know why after all those years, I decided to confide in that boyfriend. I remember being glad that I did. He was from my hometown so we went home on the weekends. One particular weekend, we went back home and I went to my mom's apartment. You will never guess who was there. *There's absolutely no way that you can guess.* It was her ex-boyfriend. *Good old Chester, Chester Child Molester!* Now what was he doing there? Why would he be there? I thought that I would never have to see that man again. *Well, well, I guess I wasn't the only one that learned to forgive. Really Ma!* Well, I left the house and got back in my car. I called my boyfriend and told him what was going on.

I found out some devastating news. My boyfriend's friend was dating my friend and she told him that my mom's ex-boyfriend fondled her when she spent the night over my house. The sad thing was that it was around the time that he molested me. She never told me that happened to her. I was furious. It was as if what happened to her was worse than what happened to me. I couldn't explain it. I called her and I told her that the man was at my mom's apartment. She told me that we needed to tell my mom. I agreed. We met up there and went in to tell my mom about this sick man. It was extremely awkward. We took her in the room right across from my mom's room where he was sitting in a chair. After holding this in for five years from my mom, she was about to find out the truth about this man.

My mom never talked to me about sex. She stayed away from any conversations that made her feel uncomfortable. I just flat out told her that when I was fourteen years old that man sitting in her room molested me. She asked me what I meant. She was looking at me like what was I talking about. My friend jumped in and bluntly told my mom that the man had sex with me. My mom's reaction was strange. I couldn't tell if she understood or didn't believe us.

My friend got frustrated and left the room. She went into my mom's room and slapped the man. She was cussing him out and going off.

What happened next was so hurtful. My mom said that we needed to leave with all that. Everything was happening so quickly that I wasn't sure who she was talking to or if she said we or he. It didn't matter though. My friend and I left. My mom didn't come after us. She wasn't that type of mother. She wasn't that type of person. We went outside where our guys were waiting on us to give the word. They were ready to fight. The good thing is there was no fight. The ex-boyfriend walked out of my mom's apartment some minutes later and got in his car. We left too. I went back to school after that weekend. I didn't bother talking to my mom. What was there to say?

I ended up not talking to my mom for nine months. She didn't call me and I certainly didn't call her. I was the child. She was my mother. I couldn't have imagined having a child and my child telling me that someone hurt them and me reacting the way that she did. I was hurt but once again my coping mechanism kicked in. I blocked it all out. When my mom and I talked again, it was because I picked up the phone and called her. *Lord, you were really doing a work in me and I thank you.* When we talked, I know you won't be surprised that my mom didn't bring up anything about what happened. *Get this right here!* To this day, over twenty years later, she has not brought it up. She has never apologized. And guess what, I was okay with that. I had forgiven all parties involved. I had definitely forgiven the guy that molested me. I had forgiven my mom. Well wait, I thought I was okay with that until I moved her into my house and we were watching a movie a couple of years ago. In the movie a young girl was being sexually abused. *Y'all, it brought up all kinds of feelings.* I was watching this movie with my mom and she was just not fazed by it.

It was sad that I had forgiven the man who molested me, but I hadn't forgiven my own mother. I prayed about it. I knew I needed to give this to God. I couldn't do it. I moved my mom into my house some years after my divorce. Why did I do this? Well, my mom has never owned a house. I bought my house at the age of twenty-six. Since my mom didn't drive, I had to help her anyway, so I thought she might as well be living with me. It wasn't a big deal to me. I loved my mom and I wanted to help her. We were good most of the time. *But let me just tell you that when the devil was busy, he was busy.* Some days I loved her but I didn't like her. I had to release this. My mom was going to be the person she was, but I knew better. I was spending way too much time with God to not start acting better. I had to be a doer of the Word and I had to heal. I had to forgive. *For real this time!* To be honest, I thought I had. What was it going to take for me to be completely healed and to fully forgive my mom?

I had counseling sessions and I talked with God which caused me to be honest with myself about how I was hurt by my mom, how I even resented her for a long list of things. I would have a great counseling session. I'd be completely fine with my mom. I would feel healed and then she would say or do something that triggered me. I would often bring up how she never said I love you, how she never showed me compassion, how she was so stern and unemotional. She would never seem phased by my words. She didn't want to talk about anything. She didn't want to talk about the past. I couldn't understand but I didn't have to. I couldn't change her, but with God helping me; I was determined to get past all of it.

The question remained: What was it going to take for me to be completely healed and to fully forgive my mom? When would it happen or would it ever happen? Well, it did. It took place twenty-two years after I told my mom what her boyfriend did to me when I was fourteen. *I know it took a while. Don't judge me.* To be completely HOT, I thought I had forgiven my mom. The reality is that just because you don't talk about the hurt and you don't face the issues, does not mean that you have forgiven the person. It still crept up. The unforgiveness, the anger, the frustration still somehow crept up. Something tragic happened that made me look at myself and look at my mom and just let go.

One day, my mom passed out in the front yard. My mom hadn't been to the doctor since I was born and I was forty-one years old. *I'm not exaggerating or being funny. This is a true story. And that tells you a lot.* She passed out in the front yard while sweeping the driveway. My teenage neighbor saw her and helped her to my other neighbor's house. I made it home and called EMS. They came and checked her out. She didn't want to go to the hospital. I didn't force her to go. I wanted it to be her decision. I knew what she had been through with her parents. That night, I asked her if she would at least go see my friend who was a nurse practitioner or my doctor. She agreed. I knew it had to be bad for my mom to agree.

The next day I went to the doctor's office to make my mom an appointment. The receptionist gave me a date that was weeks off, which concerned me. I felt in my spirit that something wasn't right with my mom and the fact that she agreed to going to the doctor meant that she knew something wasn't right with her either. While I was talking with the receptionist, God intervened. Another staff member came and told the receptionist that someone canceled their appointment. She asked me if I wanted it for my mom. I enthusiastically told her "yes". She told me that I could have the appointment but it was in an hour. I called my mom and told her to get dressed. I went and picked my mom up from home and made it back to the appointment. *Making it there on time was a miracle all in itself.*

My cousin met me there because I needed back up. I knew this wasn't going to be good. They examined my mom and her blood pressure was 235/130. They gave her a blood pressure pill and it went down some, but nowhere near enough. They gave her another blood pressure pill. Her blood pressure was higher than the last reading. They immediately sent her to the emergency room. My mom had a stroke. In fact, she had several mini strokes prior to the bigger stroke.

I remember sitting in the hospital with her and I felt guilty. I should've made her go to the doctor. I was supposed to be helping her and taking care of her. The moment that the thoughts came, they couldn't stay. God wiped them away. He knew that I loved my mom. I knew that I loved my mom. Nothing else mattered. The past didn't matter. My mom was alive. God had given her another chance. The same way that he had given me another chance. I stayed with her every day. I slept in that stupid, hard hospital chair that barely reclined. *Now, that's love!* When she was finally released from the hospital, I took my mom home. When we made it to my house, I sat her in her recliner and I hugged her. I told her that I loved her and I forgave her. She didn't say anything but at that very moment I felt like a weight was lifted off my shoulders. I felt God taking all of the anger, bitterness, frustration, hurt, and unforgiveness away.

It wasn't about her. It was truly about me. I had to forgive her for myself. I let go of it all.

God caused me to see that even though I had some hang-ups about my mom, there is actually a long list of things that I appreciate about my mom. I know it seems hard to believe after reading all the *wonderful* honest, open and transparent things I wrote about her. *I'm still hoping she never reads this. She can buy a copy but she never needs to read it. I'm just kidding, y'all.* Seriously though, the biggest thing I appreciate about my mom is how she never wavered on making me go to church. When I became a teenager, my mom did something that shocked me. She started letting me go to church with my older cousin. That one thing set the tone for my relationship with Jesus Christ. I started experiencing Christ in a new way. I fell in love with Christ. My mom gave me the most important thing in my life, she gave me God. She set the foundation for my faith.

When I went down in that watery grave, my mom was there. That was a BIG deal. You see my mom never visited other churches. She never missed her church. *I mean never.* To have her there meant a lot. Just being present was a huge thing for me because there were so many times when she wasn't there for important things in my life. My mom worked all the time. I'm grateful for her work ethic. *Shoot, like mother, like daughter.* Those are the things that I choose to focus on. It is a choice.

God revealed to me that my mom did the best that she could do. She showed me love in her own way. I couldn't imagine life in her shoes. *I don't ever want to imagine life in her shoes.* We've never sat down and talked about her childhood. We've never sat down and talked about my childhood. I'll probably never have a conversation with her where she apologizes or even acknowledges the things she has done to me and the things she hasn't done for me that hurt me. I made a decision that I was going to love her in spite of everything.

We've always been different and that's alright. My mom is an extreme introvert. I am an extreme extrovert. I'm not exaggerating. I'm an ENFP on the Myers-Briggs personality test. I have an extroverted, intuitive, feeling and perceiving personality. I am the person that never meets a stranger. I am the person starting a conversation in the elevator. I am the one writing a book and still talking to the readers. *I just can't help it. You know I was unconscious for a week so I'm making up for lost time.* My mom is really quiet. Not in the sense of the volume of her voice because she can yell for sure, but I mean she doesn't talk a lot. On the other hand, I talk all the time. *I talk all the time except for when I was unconscious. God gave everybody a break for a week but then I woke up and started back talking. Some may say I haven't stopped yet. Haters gonna hate!* But seriously though, my mom doesn't talk to you unless she has to. And even then she may try to get away with not using words.

My mom says all the time that she doesn't have friends. She's exaggerating because she has a handful of church friends that she used to sit in the back of the church with. They would laugh and joke every Sunday. Sounds like friends to me. But if you ask her if she has any friends her answer will be a firm "no". On the other hand, I have a lot of friends and associates. Another huge difference is that she doesn't drive...well wait, she can't drive. She never learned. She never learned how to do or ride anything with wheels on it. She can't skate, ride a bike, drive a car, etc. Then there's me. My oldest brother taught me how to ride his 'hand me down' big bike when I was about seven years old. My godmother started teaching me how to drive at the age of fourteen. *And if you ask me, I'm a great driver.* I love to roller skate and ice skate. Where there is an adventure to be found, I'm there. I say all of this to say that we're different, but I love her just the way she is. God gave me the heart that he gave me. I refuse to hold grudges. The enemy came in that situation to cause division. I refuse to allow the enemy to use anything. I'm not perfect and I definitely shouldn't expect anyone else to be.

Every decision I've made whether good or bad, every connection I've made whether good or bad, every encounter I've had whether good or bad, God has been right there with me. He has never left me nor forsaken me. There has been a lesson through it all. I believe that my attitude and faith helped me to build resilience. I truly believe without a shadow of doubt that God was there in the midst of every situation, every event in my life, the good and the bad. Throughout my life, I've had to truly question some things. My questions about whether God allowed me to be hurt by others led me to one definite answer. I was looking for a yes or no but it was more complex than that. A yes or no wouldn't have been sufficient enough for me anyway. God showed me that in life we all have freewill.

I had to learn that there are some decisions in life that I made that led me to some paths in my life that turned out to be more challenging. I had to learn that there are people who do bad things for their own reasons that cause other people to suffer or hurt. Whether it was by my hand or someone else's, the fact remained that God was still there. There are things that have happened to me that I don't believe He wanted to happen to me but they were allowed. I was graced to deal with them. I believe it's God who helped me get through those situations. It's God who gave me hope. It's God who brought me through horrific events in my life. It's God who equipped me with the ability to bounce back each time. I believe that God equipped me to deal with every situation I've been placed in. He is good. He is loving. He is faithful. He is kind. He is just to forgive. He is a waymaker. He is my friend. He is my heavenly father. He takes good care of me.

This process of forgiveness is a continuous process for me. The enemy tries to come for me on a daily basis. There are things that are said or done by my mom that trigger me. I can so easily start thinking about the hurt, pain, loneliness that I felt most of my life. Or I can choose to believe it's God who continues to help me forgive and move on. The latter feels a whole lot better to do. When I choose to see God, forgive and move on, my days are better. My attitude is better. I live each day happy, positive and to the fullest. Najwa Zebian said "Today I decided to forgive you. Not because you apologized, or because you acknowledged the pain that you caused me, but because my soul deserves peace".

My mom nor her ex-boyfriend ever apologized or acknowledged anything, but I decided that the best thing for me was to forgive. I realized that I don't need an apology from them. I have the power in Christ to forgive, let go and receive peace. God has given me peace that surpasses all understanding. The more that I looked to Him instead of them; I was able to let go and let God. I have chosen to give my soul peace. It's a conscious decision that I continuously make. BIG forgiveness is not easy, but it is necessary. The amazing thing is that even though it's not easy, I'm not alone. I'm not doing life alone. God is with me. God forgives us daily. We're not doing life alone. Let's extend BIG forgiveness to others.

> Forbearing one another, and forgiving one another, if any man have a quarrel against any: even as Christ forgave you, so also do ye. ~Colossians 3:13 KJV

> But if ye forgive not men their trespasses, neither will your Father forgive your trespasses. ~Matthew 6:15 NIV

Do Me A Favor

Think about how willing you are to forgive others. On a scale of 1 to 10, 1 being that you don't forgive at all and 10 being that you easily forgive others. How would you score yourself? I think I'm about an 8.5. *Shoot, it took a long time for me to get there.* Now think about someone that you need to forgive and ask God to help you forgive them. Even if the "them" is you, ask God to help you forgive yourself. If you need to, make a list of people and start checking them off. Just do it. It will be liberating. Always remember that forgiveness is for you. You are worth it. You'll thank me once you forgive "them" and the weight is lifted off of you. *You can email me to tell me I was right. I'm literally speaking from experience. Been there done that.*

Pray With Me

Father God, we come to you first to say thank you. Thank you for loving us so much that you gave your only begotten son, Jesus Christ, for us. He was the perfect sacrifice and therefore we don't have to make sacrifices in order to receive your forgiveness. Father, we're thankful that we can ask for forgiveness, repent, turn from our wicked ways and know that we are forgiven. You said that you cast it to the sea of forgetfulness. Thank you Lord. Father God, help us to give that same forgiveness to others. Father, help us to extend grace to others the same way that you extend grace to us. Help us to forgive ourselves. You're a loving and good father. You never told us that life would be fair. You never told us that trials would not come. You never said that we would not be hurt. You never said that everything would go our way. You never said that we wouldn't have difficulties. You did say that you would never leave us or forsake us. So Father, we thank you for being with us even when we're in the fire. We thank you for being with us when the enemy comes to try and steal, kill and destroy us, and everything you've called us to be. We thank you for your faithfulness even when we aren't faithful to you. For we've all fallen and come short of your glory. You keep on loving us beyond our faults and failures. Thank you Father. Thank you Father. You've been better to us than we've been to ourselves. Thank you Father. It is in the name of Jesus, we pray. Amen.

Chapter 10

BIG IDENTITY

THERE ARE SO MANY "WHYS" IN MY LIFE. THERE are so many unanswered questions. Why this? Why that? *You probably have some "Whys" about my life after making it this far in the book. I don't blame you.* I could go my entire life asking why or I could choose to just believe that God knows all and he has a purpose for me. *I'm thinking that there is a lot of purpose since I've been through all that I have. I'm just saying.* At the end of the day though, it came down to who am I? Through every experience, circumstance, failure, good decision, bad decision, accident, disappointment, good moment, bad moment, who was I? Was I a victim? *Nope.* Was I anything other than what God said I was? *Nope.* What had I learned from my story? My story is my testimony. It has shaped me. It has changed me. What about you and your story?

I chose to believe that my life was not just full of obstacles and tests. My life was full of ordained, orchestrated testimonies. I have been through the fiery furnace and the only thing burned were the ropes that had me bound. It's not over but even now I know that God had purpose in everything He orchestrated. He even used the things that I put my hands in, that He didn't orchestrate, for purpose. He even went a step further and used the bad things that were done to me by others for purpose. I believe He has a part in every area of my life. I realized that I went through so much more because I am called to so much more.

Over the years, one of the highlights of my life has been working with young people. There is something about spending time with young people that has helped me to feel younger, more energetic. There is an energy that I receive from hanging with them. People tell me that I don't look my age. I like to think that comes from spending time with young people. *Who needs anti-aging cream when I can just go kick it and laugh with teenagers!* I've volunteered in youth ministry over the years. For well over a decade, I have led a youth Exploring group for fourteen to twenty year olds. I've been blessed to have impacted over 1,500 students who were interested in healthcare careers in the many years that I led the program. These young people brought so much into my life. While *somewhat* teaching, encouraging and inspiring youth, in actuality I've learned a lot from them. I've learned a lot from the young girls that I help lead at my church. They too have taught me so much. *Some of the things I've learned I should have just left alone. Some of the things that I picked up, I should have put them back down.*

I'll keep it HOT and let you in on what I picked up from the students. One day I heard a word that drew me in and wouldn't let me go. I could not stop saying it. *Ratchet.* Yes, *ratchet.* Out of all the words in the world, my students were using the slang word *ratchet.* Everyone that knows me knows I say this word all the time. I use it when I'm describing myself, when I'm explaining my past, when I'm warning people that I could get foolish. *One of those "Lord, have mercy on me" moments.* The sad thing was I wasn't fully familiar with the word because I didn't know there was a whole song that I hadn't even heard. I was going around saying how ratchet I was and could possibly be again if provoked.

BIG IDENTITY

You can act like you never had a moment that you weren't very proud of but I'm just speaking the truth. We have all had a ratchet moment or even moments. Maybe your list isn't as long as mine, but like my sister's grandma says "keep on living".

There honestly may have been some times that weren't my proudest moments. *Okay, there is no "may". We all know there are several times just in this book alone that weren't my proudest moments. No judgment.* Well, guess what, the Bible is full of people who had ratchet moments. I am not the one to call anybody out but come on. We have Eve *(SMH)*, David *(SMH)*, Peter *(SMH)*, etc. The list goes on and on and on. I definitely would have been on that list if I was alive back then. I'm not perfect. No one is but Christ. Thank God for Him. He paved the way for my redemption. God showed me something one day that blew my mind. He showed me that in the world, I was ratchet but with Him, I'm RATCHET. He showed me that the life that I've lived, the storms I've been through, the good times where I laughed and the bad times when I cried, help shape me into who I am today.

Who am I? I am RATCHET. I realized when it all comes down to it, I'm RATCHET. I am **R**edeemed. I am **A**nointed. I am **T**enacious. I am **C**hosen. I am **H**ealed. I am **E**quipped. I am **T**hankful. With me knowing that I'm RATCHET, it has helped me to walk in freedom. I am able to have a mindset focused on God. The miracles He's done in my life helped me to grow closer to Him. Put your focus on God. With God, we are all RATCHET. Just say it with me, my name is_____ and I'm RATCHET. If you don't want to say you're RATCHET, it's okay. *You'll come around. You probably didn't see that coming, but at this point I'm capable of anything.* Don't be too surprised. God has a way of using the least expected things and people to show us more of Him. Just remember:

Redeemed
Anointed
Tenacious
Chosen
Healed
Equipped
Thankful

If you live your life being redeemed, anointed, tenacious, chosen, healed, equipped, thankful, there is no devil that can stop you from all that God has for you. The enemy will try but you will be able to stand strong knowing that God is on your side. The weapon may form but I am a believer that it won't prosper. There may be times that you mess up but just know that you are redeemed. You were bought with a price. Jesus Christ paid that price on a cross for you and me. There may be times when you don't feel like you can do something but you are anointed to do whatever God has called you to. There is a God-given, kingdom assignment that needs to be fulfilled. There may be times when you have to remember that you are Chosen. God created you. You have the characteristics of Christ. You represent him. You are chosen for a purpose. You are chosen for His purpose. You have to know that Christ chose you before you chose Him. He sees you just as you are and loves you just as you are. When you don't think that you are qualified, remember that you are His child and He loves you, He chose you and He was intentional when He created you.

There may be times when you're sick or you have been given an unfavorable diagnosis, remember that you are healed. I've learned that it doesn't matter what it looks like in the natural. God is always working in the supernatural making things work out for your good. Believe that you are healed. There may be times when you feel insufficient, remember that you are equipped. God has given you everything you need. He is your provider. If you have lack in your life, know that He will provide. He's equipped you. Believe that He will meet your needs. There have been times in my life where I thought I didn't have enough. I thought I wasn't smart enough. I thought I wasn't brave enough. I thought I wasn't strong enough. I thought I wasn't pretty enough. I thought I wasn't good enough. *Well, the list is long and it continues, but you get it.* I had to learn that I have all that I need. I just need to tap into what God has given me.

He provides resources (finances, people, etc.). He provides confidence. He provides courage. He provides strength. He provides wisdom. There will be times when you don't feel like going on. The times when you may feel like giving up on what God is calling you to do or continue doing, know that you are tenacious. Be persistent. Keep on keeping on. God has given you a drive to continue. He wants you to reach your goals. He wants to use you. Do not get weary in your well doing. How do I know any of this? How can I write this with all this confidence? I believe so strongly because of the confidence I have in God. Yes, I humbly say that I have a lot of confidence in myself. *Some may say sometimes too much confidence, but to each their own.* The confidence that I have in myself is nothing compared to the confidence I have in God. I know and believe that he wants to use you because he used me. I was the lowercase ratchet, the worldly ratchet person but be transformed by the renewing of my mind. There is something that happened to me when I began to spend more time with the Lord.

The Holy Spirit is my helper and was at full attention when I started putting God first. *I can still be that ratchet person without the Holy Spirit keeping me in check. I've had people tell me it doesn't take all that going to church, being a part of several ministries, listening to worship music all day, and reading the Bible all the time. I think* to myself they have no idea what a mess I am in the flesh. *For me, it takes all that and some on a daily basis.* I thank God that the spirit is strong even when the flesh is weak. The thing is that when I start my day off focusing on God, He is able to work through me in ways I couldn't even imagine. If God can use me, David, Eve, Peter, Moses, and all the other people that have had a failed, ratchet moment(s), I believe that God can absolutely use anyone.

To me there's no shadow of a doubt that God saved me in that car accident. It's unexplainable to me how I could survive. It's unexplainable to me how an off duty officer who never went that way home, went that way that night. It's unexplainable that an unknown guy helped get me out of a car submerged underwater and then disappeared. *No one even remembers how he looks. Really!* It's unexplainable to me how my neck was broken to the point that two bones had to be replaced and fused, but I'm not paralyzed from my neck down. It's definitely unexplainable to me how I was underwater for over ten minutes and I didn't drown. *As you can see, I didn't die.* It's unexplainable that I didn't have brain damage like the neurosurgeon warned my mom. It's even unexplainable to me how I went to bed one night without the activity of my left arm and I woke up the next morning and it was fully functioning. It's unexplainable to me that the negative effects that could have happened to me after being sexually abused at fourteen years old didn't happen. It's unexplainable to me how I moved in with a stranger who ended up being the connection to meeting my dad. *Remember I thought he was dead.*

I believe that God is always in the midst of the unexplainable. I believe He does the unexplainable. He can do the impossible and I'm living proof of that. He can cause a setback to be the place of your bounce back. He is God all by Himself and He can work in amazing ways. He has no limits. It is up to us to see all the things, little and big things, that He is doing.

I've lived a life full of *Couldas*. I *coulda* been dead. It *coulda* been worse. If you look at your life, you will see that things could have been different. We all have *couldas*. There is not one person alive that doesn't have something that could have happened to them. There can always be something worse. At times I've thought I was at my lowest point but I realized it could always be worse. *You made it this far so just one last quick story.* I was determined to never cause a car accident. *Notice I said "cause".* I've been in a couple of accidents but I'm proud to say it was never my fault. Well, never say never because I was in my first at fault car accident at the age of forty. I hit a young lady. To make matters worse she had kids in the car. Thankfully, no one was hurt. *In all honesty, the Holy Spirit told me to not make that left turn because I couldn't see clear. See what disobedience got me. Hard head makes a soft behind.* Well, it wasn't a bad car accident but very well could have been. I actually didn't get upset at myself. I didn't panic and worry. I had peace when I realized that it could have been so much worse. No one was hurt and we *coulda* been injured. I had insurance and I *coulda* not. I had the money for my deductible and I *coulda* been broke. From the time that it happened, I realized that it *coulda* just been so much worse.

My attitude lined up with my positive thoughts. My attitude lined up with seeing God's grace and mercy in the situation. There was no need to get upset. I knew it was my fault. I didn't get dramatic *(which if you know me, you know I can and would)*. I was alright. Whether we choose to believe that it is God who steps in, is completely up to us. I decided that in my life, I'm going to look for the *Couldas*. By looking at what could have happened if God had not stepped in to protect me, save me, keep me, has helped me to be more positive. I live a good life because I live a grateful life. I'm grateful for the *Couldas*.

How do you get to the place of being able to embrace *Couldas*, have peace that surpasses all understanding, and look at life in a more positive way no matter what you're facing? For me, it's been simple. I started focusing on God immediately when I wake up. Every morning, I say thank you Lord for another day like my mom used to do when I was growing up. I was acknowledging God first thing and that was enough for me. *I'm just not a morning person!* Well, something happened to me the more that I was reading His word and listening to messages. I began to spend more time with God in the mornings. *Look who turned into a morning person. Well, sometimes.*

As I began to spend more time with Him, doors started opening for me to lead more in ministry. One day my cousin's pastor, who didn't know me, asked me to lead a Bible study. I agreed knowing that this man of God had to hear from God because he didn't even know me. He gave me the subject which was Spiritual Meditation: Getting Closer to God. *When he said the subject, I thought "You gotta be more careful, Liz. You should've asked about the topic first."* He followed up with telling me that I needed to be doing it before teaching it. I'm not a pastor. I didn't feel qualified, but for some reason, I had an assignment (one that I felt was from God).

I studied and researched. I realized that the topic that I was given was about putting God FIRST and getting closer to Him. I needed that. I learned that it is a continuous journey. My relationship with God is ongoing. I have to keep spending time with Him in order for our relationship to grow and not falter. When I look back over my life, I can tell you the seasons in my life where I was spending more time with God and when I wasn't. *You probably can tell too after reading this.*

BIG IDENTITY

Time with God is so important. God wants us to search His word and find out what He says about us. Everything God created is good. I have some good news. We made the list. He created us and as our heavenly father, He created us and said that we were very good. Genesis 1:31 KJV says "Then God saw everything that He had made, and indeed it was very good. And the evening and the morning were the sixth day." He created us in his own image. His desire is for us to know Him and to love Him. He wants us to live in peace. In my opinion, He wants us to be RATCHET. God wants us to find our identity in Him and Him alone. It's a BIG identity. When it's all said and done, I live BIG no matter what comes my way. I am BIG. I will forever believe it's God in every situation working all things together for my good because I love Him and I am called according to His purpose. Are you ready to live BIG?

> Therefore if any man be in Christ, he is a new creature: old things are passed away; behold, all things are become new. ~2 Corinthians 5:17 KJV

> For we are his workmanship, created in Christ Jesus unto good works, which God hath before ordained that we should walk in them. ~Ephesians 2:10 KJV

> And God said unto Moses, I Am That I Am: and he said, thus shalt thou say unto the children of Israel, I Am hath sent me unto you. ~Exodus 3:14 KJV

> But as many as received him, to them gave he power to become the sons of God, even to them that believe on his name. ~John 1:12

Do Me A Favor

Please do me one last favor. Choose to think BIG. Choose to live BIG. Believe it's God. Live each day knowing that you are able to experience and walk in His promises. You are able to receive His miracles, wait on His timing, be victorious in His battles, pray for His wisdom, rely on His divine plans, accept His mercy, receive His healing, give and receive His forgiveness and take on His identity. Now that's BIG!

Pray With Me

Father God, the Great I am! Holy, loving, gracious, merciful God, thank you for blessing us with life. We know that every good and perfect gift comes from you. We thank you Father God that you are everything we need and so much more. You are Jehovah Jireh and there is no other provider that can take care of us like you do. Thank you for a relationship with you through your Son, Jesus Christ. We thank you for the Holy Spirit abiding in us, interceding for us, working in us. You knew us while we were still in our mother's womb. You know every hair on our head. Please help us to strive daily to know you better and to love you more. We long to have a deeper relationship with you each day. Show us how you are using everything in our lives for our good even when it doesn't look like it. Help us to see you in every situation in our lives. We know that if we put our focus on you, we can see things the way you see them. If we fix our eyes on you, we can make it through anything. We commit this day to you. We commit our lives to you. We commit our stories to you to be used for your glory, to be used for the upbuilding of your kingdom. It is in the name of Jesus, we pray. Amen.

    Now Father God, I pray for each reader that has picked up this book. I pray that they have felt your holy presence while reading.

I pray that you will bless them in a mighty way. I pray that the gifts and talents that you have blessed them with will be identified and magnified, in the name of Jesus. I pray that they will live life to the fullest knowing that you are with them and that you will never leave them nor forsake them because they are your children. There is nothing they can do to separate them from your love. Help them to feel that love every day and every moment of their lives. Father, they are who you say they are and anything contrary to that is a lie. Help them to not believe the lies and schemes of the enemy. Keep them rooted in you. Keep them rooted in your word. Keep their minds stayed on you. Help them to live BIG and know that you are the one, true, living God and there is no other. You are God and you are God all by yourself. Help your believers to keep believing. It is in Your Son, Our Savior, Jesus Christ name, I pray. Amen!

AFTERWORD

As I come to a close, I am leaving you with a lot of hope. I hope that you have been inspired by my life, my testimonies. I hope that you have found hope, joy, peace and even some humor. Mostly, I hope that you have found a new appreciation for your own life, appreciation for trials that you may have faced in life. I hope that you have found a new appreciation for things that happened in your life that the enemy wants to hang over your head and make you feel ashamed, defeated or less than. Those aren't just things that the enemy can use. They are testimonies that you can use to give God glory. My prayer is that you are inspired to share your testimony with those individuals that God leads you to. If God is stirring up something in you, take on the assignment. He has created each of us for His glory. Each morning God wakes us up with purpose. Each morning new mercy and grace is given to us to accomplish his plan for our lives. Be obedient and walk into all that God has for you. *Even if it's writing a book that you don't want to write, but you know you have to.*

I know through writing this book that God is indeed the author and the finisher. When I was close to finishing *That's BIG*, God made it clear to me that I was to include an invitation to receive Christ. Maybe after reading this book, you realize that you want to know Christ or you want a deeper relationship with Him. If you feel that you want to know Christ or maybe you are a backslider that wants to come back to Him, here is your opportunity.

First of all, it's important that you know that Jesus loves you. His grace and mercy extends beyond any sins you've knowingly or unknowingly committed. God loves and cares for you so much that He sent His only begotten Son (Jesus) into this sinful world to pay the price and penalty for our sins. What Jesus did gave us an opportunity to have an eternal life. Don't let this opportunity pass you by. Accept Jesus Christ as your Lord and Savior today.

Some people think it's difficult to come to Christ or even to come back to him, but really it's as simple as repenting (asking God for forgiveness) of all your sins and believing in your heart that Jesus is the Son of God. *I've had to do this a time or two or three or four.* Pray a prayer of faith, ask God to forgive you and to come into your heart, and fill you with his Holy Spirit. God is faithful and just, so He will be right there ready to receive you as his own as soon as you ask and are ready to begin your journey with Him, right where you are. You don't have to wait until you get better or until you change. God does the changing. Just surrender. It doesn't matter where you are in your life at this point. Even if the Lord has to reach way down, He can and will still pick you up. *I'm a living witness.* Jesus can be your Lord and Savior right now. Just take a moment, pause where you are, and pray this simple prayer:

Dear Lord, I am a sinner and I acknowledge that I need you to come in my life. Wash me and cleanse me of all my sins so that I can be in right standing with you. I believe in my heart that Jesus Christ is your son. I accept Him as my personal Lord and Savior. Come into my heart and fill me with your Spirit so that I can live for you. It is in the name of Jesus. Amen.

If you have prayed this prayer in faith and have truly received Christ, you have now become a child of God! The angels in Heaven are rejoicing at this good news! Nothing compares to being a child of the Most High!

The next step for you is to find a Bible-believing and Bible-teaching church and start attending so that you may grow in the knowledge of Christ and become strong in the faith. I realized that if I had not been led to the churches and ministries that I'm a part of, I definitely wouldn't have grown in my relationship with Christ.

I wish you all the best in your new walk and know that with God on your side and with your willing heart, nothing is impossible. The enemy has been defeated. God is more powerful than the enemy will ever be. Remember that God loves you with an everlasting, unconditional love!

Be blessed. Keep striving. Believe It's God.

ABOUT THE AUTHOR/VESSEL

ELIZABETH WILLIAMS HAS DEVOTED HER LIFE to service: serving God and people. Her mission is to encourage others and bring God glory through sharing her testimony of how God literally brought her back to life after a traumatic car accident. She was born and raised in Montgomery, Alabama by her single mother. Elizabeth received her B.A. in Communication and Information Sciences from the University of Alabama in 2003. She is a marketing and communications professional with sixteen years of experience in community engagement for a local hospital system. Elizabeth received her certification in life coaching from International Association of Professions Career College in 2021. She serves as the Executive Board Chair for Girls on the Run South Central Alabama. Elizabeth volunteers with several local nonprofit organizations. She has been recognized by the Boy Scouts of America for her distinguished service by being named as one of the recipients of the National Silver Beaver Award. She volunteers at True Divine Baptist Church, in the girls' ministry, greeting ministry and health ministry. She is also a member of True Divine's Leaders Investing For Tomorrow (LIFT) Leadership and Mentor Program. Elizabeth is a lay coordinator for Gathered by Grace Ministry. She also serves on the Gathered by Grace Connection Team. One of Elizabeth's favorite things to do is travel. As a motivational speaker, she loves the opportunity to travel and speak at churches, conferences, nonprofit organizations and schools. She is the owner of MindingYourLiz. Above everything, Elizabeth is a Christian and a survivor who lives and thinks BIG.

To find out more information about Elizabeth and her journey, go to www.thatsbigbook.com. If you are interested in booking her for a speaking engagement, please email your request to thatsbigbook@gmail.com.

CPSIA information can be obtained
at www.ICGtesting.com
Printed in the USA
BVHW071537020223
657731BV00006B/252